The Israelites

The Emergence of Man

The Israelites

by the Editors
of TIME-LIFE BOOKS

TIME-LIFE BOOKS
New York

TIME-LIFE BOOKS

FOUNDER: Henry R. Luce 1898-1967

Editor-in-Chief: Hedley Donovan
Chairman of the Board: Andrew Heiskell
President: James R. Shepley
Group Vice President: Rhett Austell

Vice Chairman: Roy E. Larsen

MANAGING EDITOR: Jerry Korn
Assistant Managing Editors: Ezra Bowen,
David Maness, Martin Mann, A. B. C. Whipple
Planning Director: Oliver E. Allen
Art Director: Sheldon Cotler
Chief of Research: Beatrice T. Dobie
Director of Photography: Melvin L. Scott
Senior Text Editors: Diana Hirsh, William Frankel
Assistant Art Director: Arnold C. Holeywell
Assistant Chief of Research: Myra Mangan

PUBLISHER: Joan D. Manley
General Manager: John D. McSweeney
Business Manager: Nicholas J. C. Ingleton
Sales Director: Carl G. Jaeger
Promotion Director: Paul R. Stewart
Public Relations Director: Nicholas Benton

THE EMERGENCE OF MAN

Editorial Staff for The Israelites:
EDITOR: Charles Osborne
Assistant Editor: Johanna Zacharias
Text Editor: Anne Horan
Picture Editor: Jean Tennant
Designer: Albert Sherman
Staff Writers: Marion Buhagiar, Sara M. Clark, Jill Spiller, Eve Wengler
Chief Researcher: Peggy Bushong
Researchers: Josephine Reidy, Constance R. Roosevelt, Josephine Burke,
Karen M. Bates, Ellie McGrath, Joann W. McQuiston, Carolyn Stallworth,
Jean Stratton

EDITORIAL PRODUCTION
Production Editor: Douglas B. Graham
Assistant Production Editors: Gennaro C. Esposito,
Feliciano Madrid
Quality Director: Robert L. Young
Assistant Quality Director: James J. Cox
Copy Staff: Eleanore W. Karsten (chief), Charles Blackwell,
Elaine Pearlmutter, Florence Keith, Pearl Sverdlin
Picture Department: Dolores A. Littles, Marianne Dowell
Traffic: Carmen McLellan

Valuable assistance was given by the following departments and
individuals of Time Inc.: Editorial Production, Norman Airey; Library,
Benjamin Lightman; Picture Collection, Doris O'Neil; Photographic
Laboratory, George Karas; TIME-LIFE News Service, Murray J. Gart;
Correspondents Elaine Farbenbloom and Marlin Levin (Jerusalem),
Margot Hapgood and Dorothy Bacon (London), Maria Vincenza Aloisi
and Josephine du Brusle (Paris), Ann Natanson (Rome), Elisabeth
Kraemer (Bonn) and Traudl Lessing (Vienna).

The Consultants: BARUCH A. LEVINE, a specialist in Biblical studies and the history of monotheism, is Professor of Hebrew and Chairman of the Department of Near Eastern Languages and Literatures at New York University. He is a frequent contributor to scholarly journals and reference works in both English and Hebrew. His book, In the Presence of the Lord: A Study of Cult and Some Cultic Terms in Ancient Israel, was published in 1974. JAMES BENNET PRITCHARD, Professor of Religious Thought and Curator of Biblical Archeology at the University of Pennsylvania, was President of the Archeological Institute of America until 1974. He has participated in excavations in Jordan and Lebanon. His published works include Ancient Near Eastern Texts Relating to the Old Testament and Archeology and the Old Testament.

The Cover: At sunrise in the broken, mountainous country of the southern Sinai Peninsula, an Israelite elder pauses to survey the terrain ahead. He and his followers are among the hundreds of Israelite families who, according to the Bible, escaped from bondage in Egypt around 1225 B.C. and followed Moses across the desert to the Promised Land of Canaan. The figures were painted by artist Burt Silverman against a photographic background that includes the mountain range of which Jebel Musa is part. The peak traditionally has been identified as Mount Sinai where, as the Book of Exodus recounts, Moses received the Ten Commandments.

Editor's Note: As the text of this volume relates, the personal god of Abraham was originally just one more deity in the vast pantheons of the ancients. It was not until centuries had passed that men identified Him as God, the familiar central figure of monotheism. This book deals with the anthropological and historical origins of the Israelites, and the paramount role religion played in their emergence. To maintain this historical perspective, the editors have chosen to refer to the tribal god of the Israelites with a lowercase initial letter; a capital letter is used when the word occurs in a passage quoted or paraphrased from the Bible.

Contents

Introduction

Of all the ancient peoples of the Near East, the Israelites are the most familiar to us. The sense of recognition is due primarily to the wide distribution of the Hebrew Bible, which has been translated from the original into scores of languages. It is sacred writ to both Christian and Jew, has a role in the Islamic tradition, and has thereby become imbedded in the humanistic heritage of civilization.

Still, though the Bible remains the principal source of knowledge about the Israelites, new approaches to its study have altered our conceptions of this ancient people and our understanding of the book itself. Not too long ago, continuing close examination of the Biblical texts was prompted in the main by theological concerns. But the new availability of historical materials—written sources, artifacts and structural remains, all hidden since antiquity and uncovered by modern archeologists—has revolutionized our perceptions of the texts.

According to Biblical tradition, ancestral patriarchs and their nomadic clans residing in Canaan were the first to enter into a covenant with the god of Israel, who promised Canaan to their descendants. Driven by natural disasters and the nomadic habit of constant movement, the patriarchal clans went down to Egypt and sojourned there for at least several generations, during which time they were reduced to servitude. Finally, the god of their fathers remembered his promise to the patriarchs and sent Moses to lead them out of bondage, in the process demonstrating his supremacy over the gods of powerful Egypt. Thereupon, their god revealed his law to the Israelites at Sinai, renewed the covenant and insisted on exclusive worship.

The next important stage in the development of monotheism came in the Eighth Century B.C. Prophets like Isaiah, reacting to the expansion of the Assyrian Empire, asserted that the god of the Israelites was responsible for all the epochal episodes of that period; that he ruled the Assyrians as well as the Israelites—an interpretation of international events that cast the Israelite god for the first time as a universal deity.

Not surprisingly, the closer incidents recorded in the Bible fall in relation to our own times, the easier it is to establish their historical validity. The wanderings of Abraham and his progeny—the patriarchal founders of the Israelite tradition—are difficult to trace with precision, but there is little doubt that they did live in Canaan. The Israelite sojourn in Egypt is somewhat easier to corroborate, through records from Egypt itself and neighboring territories. Settlement in Canaan after the Exodus can be dated fairly accurately to the beginning of the Iron Age, around 1200 B.C. Within perhaps two centuries from that time, the confederation of the Israelite tribes had given rise to a united monarchy, with Jerusalem as its capital. That central political structure was not to last however. Soon it divided into two kingdoms—Israel in the north and Judah in the south, with Jerusalem still its capital. By the first quarter of the Sixth Century B.C., both kingdoms had fallen to foreign invaders, bringing to a close the Israelite rule in Canaan after about 600 years.

The ideas and institutions that emerged during that span have had a profound influence on the course of human history. The Bible reveals just how they developed through several stages, how the Israelites gave expression to their religious conception in worship and celebration, and how they understood their origins as a nation and the birth of their religious way of life.

The people among whom this deeply revolutionary body of ideas flowered were not wealthy or powerful, even by the standards of their own day. Other contemporary peoples—notably the Assyrians and Babylonians, who swept the Israelites into exile and ended the first and truly formative stage of their history—are primarily interesting for their fabled riches and their recorded feats of empire building. But the chronicles of the Israelites are fascinating because out of their relatively humble daily lives developed the ideas that became mankind's vision of a world at peace and its hope of eternal redemption.

Baruch A. Levine
Professor of Hebrew
Chairman, Department of
Near Eastern Languages and Literatures
New York University

Chapter One: Wanderers Who Forged a Faith

In the year 597 B.C. the religious leader who has come down in Biblical tradition as the prophet Jeremiah had every reason to view the future of his people with great pessimism. The Israelites appeared to be doomed. Jeremiah, a preacher from a hilltop village outside Jerusalem, was a witness as thousands of his countrymen, the elite of the city, assembled in Jerusalem for a journey into exile, a terrible march that would take them several hundred miles across the desert to Babylonia. They moved off to the sounds of lamentations, accompanied by the braying of donkeys, the tinkling of bronze bells, the creaking of cart wheels. The Babylonians were breaking up their kingdom, taking over their cities, rooting them out of house and home, driving them off their land. Jeremiah could not observe this cataclysm without a reaction so powerful and so far-reaching that the world still lives with its effects.

For all Israelites it was an article of faith that the land belonged to them by the terms of a sacred covenant made with the Almighty by their forefathers. But to Jeremiah it seemed that more than the land was at stake; he feared that his people's religion would be destroyed under pressures from the polytheistic world into which they were being forced. At home in Jerusalem, there was but one temple. In Babylon, the capital of Babylonia, there would be many, signifying the worship of a profusion of gods, each assigned a different function in the intricate plan that

An early representation of the Ark of the Covenant on a wheeled cart, this section of a frieze was found in the ruins of a Third Century A.D. synagogue near the Sea of Galilee. The ark, the shrine that traditionally housed the tablets inscribed with the Israelites' sacred laws, had to be mobile because in the early days the people were constantly on the move.

sustained the universe and oversaw the lives of men.

Jeremiah himself remained behind in Jerusalem, probably because the conquerors did not consider a mere country preacher sufficiently threatening to warrant removing him. But leaving Jeremiah behind was ill-conceived; his influence was profound. Tradition has it that, as the banished Israelites made ready to leave, he wrote a priestly exhortation for them to ponder on their way. In words whose eloquence has reverberated through the centuries, he reminded them of the tenets of monotheism, the worship of one god. His purpose was to save those exiled thousands and their religion.

On the face of it, Jeremiah's message to the Israelites was a simple scolding. He accused them of lapses of faith: "The sins you have committed in the sight of God," he said, "are the cause of your being led away captive."

But buried in the prophet's words was a note of hope. If punishment followed upon misbehavior, the converse might also be true: good behavior should bring reward. That concept, in turn, suggested that every individual had a role in working out his own fate. In effect, Jeremiah was urging each Israelite to accept moral responsibility for his own acts as a prerequisite to coping with misfortune.

The definition of proper behavior sprang from one key precept, and Jeremiah added words of advice for the grim days ahead. "Now in Babylon," he went on, "you will see carried on men's shoulders gods made of silver, gold and wood, which fill the heathen with awe. Be careful, then, never to imitate these foreigners; do not be carried away by their gods when you see them in the midst of a procession of worshippers. But say in your hearts, 'To thee alone, Lord, is worship due.' '' After dealing at some length with the evils of Babylon, Jeremiah concluded: "These wooden gods of theirs, plated with gold and silver, give no better protection than a scarecrow in a plot of cucumbers." And Jeremiah proclaimed the existence of a god far more encompassing and more efficacious than any man-made figurine.

Most important was the phrase "say in your hearts." The effect was to lay down a precept by which much of civilization is still guided. It implied that—no matter how perplexing the trials of life —there was a personal link between the Israelites' god and his believers. It bypassed the trappings of temples, the intervention of priests, the pomp of ritual procession and provided a two-way line of communication with a deity whose vision reached into the most intimate corners of every believer's life.

Behind Jeremiah's words was a profound revolution in man's way of thinking about himself and his relationship to the universe. This radical change was embodied in the belief that a single, unifying divine spirit stands behind the world's creation—allpowerful, all-knowing, present everywhere, perfect. Though the journey on which the Israelites embarked at the dawn of the Sixth Century B.C. was, essentially, a closing episode of their political life in the ancient world, the event also marked a new beginning: the faith that they carried with them into Babylonia was to become their legacy to human culture.

In the two and a half millennia that have elapsed since the Babylonian exile, monotheism has traveled around the world. It has grown into an elaborate corpus of beliefs that virtually defies exhaustive definition. It has been embellished upon, pared down, dressed up again and fought over ad infinitum. Many

An Israelite Chronology

c. 1900-1300 B.C.
Possible time span of Biblical patriarchal age.
c. 1300 B.C.
Period of bondage in Egypt.
c. 1225 B.C.
Exodus from Egypt through desert wilderness.
c. 1200 B.C.
Tribes settle in Canaan; age of judges begins.
c. 1190 B.C.
Philistines invade and take over Canaan's southern coast.
c. 1050 B.C.
Philistines capture Ark of the Covenant.
c. 1025 B.C.
Saul annointed first king of the Israelites; wins back some territory from Philistines.
c. 1000 B.C.
David becomes king, expels Philistines, expands Israelite dominion, establishes Jerusalem as national capital and brings to it the Ark of the Covenant.
961 B.C.
Solomon inherits throne; beginning of Israel's most prosperous and powerful period.
922 B.C.
Solomon dies. Israelite nation splits into northern kingdom of Israel, with first capital at Shechem, and southern kingdom of Judah, centered at Jerusalem.
876 B.C.
King Omri of Israel founds new capital at Samaria.
842 B.C.
Queen Jezebel of Israel imposes cult of Baal and the people revolt. Weakened by internal turmoil, Israel loses land to the Aramaeans.
c. 750 B.C.
Prophets Amos and Hosea decry exploitation of the poor by the wealthy of Israel.
738 B.C.
Assyria exacts heavy tribute from Israel.
721 B.C.
Assyrians conquer Israel and deport many of its people. Judah becomes a vassal state under the Assyrians and is forced to pay tribute.
715 B.C.
Hezekiah assumes throne of Judah, purifies religion of Assyrian influences.
687 B.C.
Assyrians besiege Jerusalem.
640-609 B.C.
King Josiah of Judah wins some territory from Assyria, whose power is declining.
597 B.C.
Babylonians capture Jerusalem and deport King Jehoiachin.
587 B.C.
Babylonians destroy Jerusalem, causing the collapse of the kingdom of Judah.

peoples in many places have developed other ways of dealing with man's spiritual perplexities. But of the seven or eight major religions that claim the allegiance of mankind today, monotheism forms the basis of three: Christianity, Islam, and Judaism—the direct descendant of the Israelites' religion.

This is the story of how that concept evolved: of the people who developed it in those long, tumultuous years before the exile from Jerusalem; of the heritage, centuries in the making, that the exhortation of Jeremiah helped to preserve.

Who, then, were the Israelites? How did they come to believe as they did?

They were a Near Eastern people who emerged on the stage of history some time in the Second Millennium B.C. Beginning as a collection of nomadic families, and then merging into a confederation of tribes, they settled down to farm, built cities and then formed a kingdom that fostered the elements of higher civilization: wide-ranging trade, monumental building, writing, codes of law. By Jeremiah's time, the religion of the Israelites had been forming for at least 700 years, perhaps for more than a thousand.

To answer the question of how they came to think and believe as they did it is necessary to go back even further, to about the dawn of the Second Millennium B.C. The answers—many of them still unsettled and shrouded in mysteries—come from the efforts of many scholars in different fields: archeologists who have dug up the artifacts of ancient civilizations long buried under the earth-covered mounds of the Near East; historians who have analyzed the ancient legal, literary and commercial records of those ancient civilizations; and scholars

of the Bible, that enduring book in which the Israelites themselves recorded their own history, their laws and the articles of their faith.

The Bible has survived from antiquity as living tradition. For generation after generation, since it was first compiled in Hebrew, the faithful of the three monotheistic religions—and challenging doubters as well—have mined the Bible, quoted its precepts, translated it, and based volumes of their prose, their poetry and their civil as well as religious laws on it. In the process they have added new interpretations and obscured old ones, immensely complicating the task of sifting truth from legend. Archeological and historical finds, on the other hand, whether stumbled upon or diligently sought out, have recovered evidence, often of beliefs and practices that had been long forgotten. Thus archeology, in peeling away the layers of more recent ideas, has enabled scholars to superimpose historical evaluations on Biblical traditions so long taken for granted.

For centuries tradition held, among other things, that the Bible told an accurate chronological story, recounting the history of the Israelites from the creation of the world. Of the 39 books that make up the Old Testament (the section of the Bible that antedates the Christian Era, with which the New Testament begins), the first five were long thought to have been written by Moses, who delivered the Israelites out of slavery in Egypt. He gave them the Ten Commandments and led them to the threshold of the land promised to the patriarchs of their tribal family—Abraham, Isaac and Jacob—by their god, Yahweh. (The name was written YHWH, which in the Middle Ages was mistranslated from Hebrew as Jehovah.) The remaining 34 books were thought to have

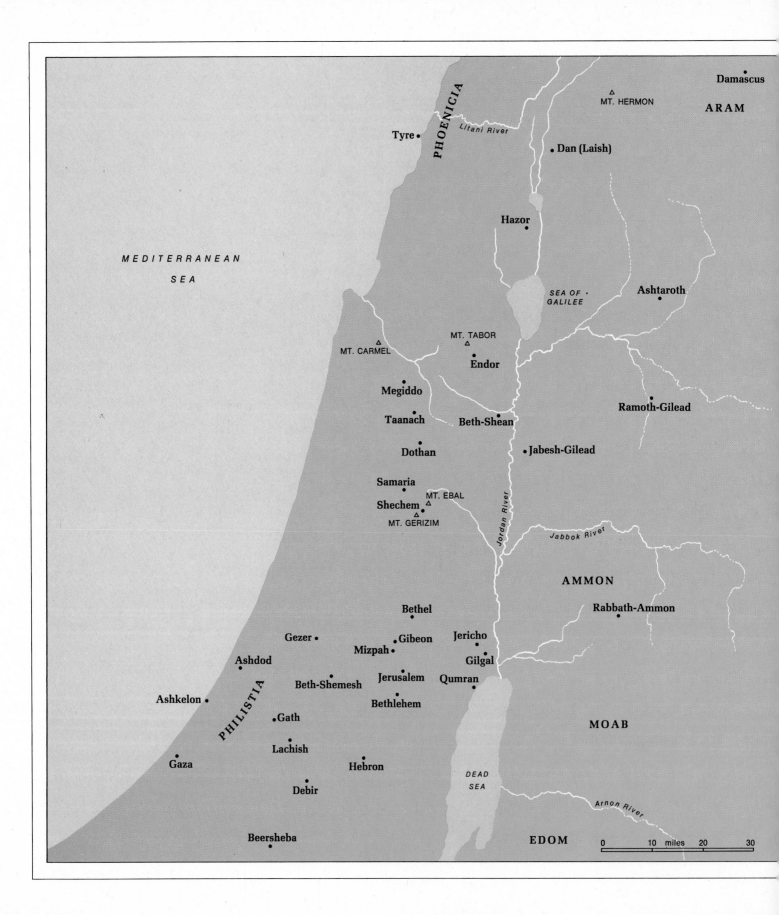

Damascus

PHOENICIA

MT. HERMON

ARAM

Tyre

Litani River

Dan (Laish)

Hazor

MEDITERRANEAN
SEA

SEA OF
GALILEE

Ashtaroth

MT. TABOR

MT. CARMEL

Endor

Megiddo

Ramoth-Gilead

Taanach

Beth-Shean

Dothan

Jabesh-Gilead

Samaria

Shechem

MT. EBAL

MT. GERIZIM

Jordan River

Jabbok River

AMMON

Bethel

Rabbath-Ammon

Gezer

Gibeon

Jericho

Mizpah

Gilgal

Ashdod

Jerusalem

Beth-Shemesh

Qumran

Ashkelon

Bethlehem

PHILISTIA

Gath

MOAB

Lachish

Gaza

DEAD
SEA

Hebron

Debir

Arnon River

Beersheba

EDOM

0   10   miles   20   30

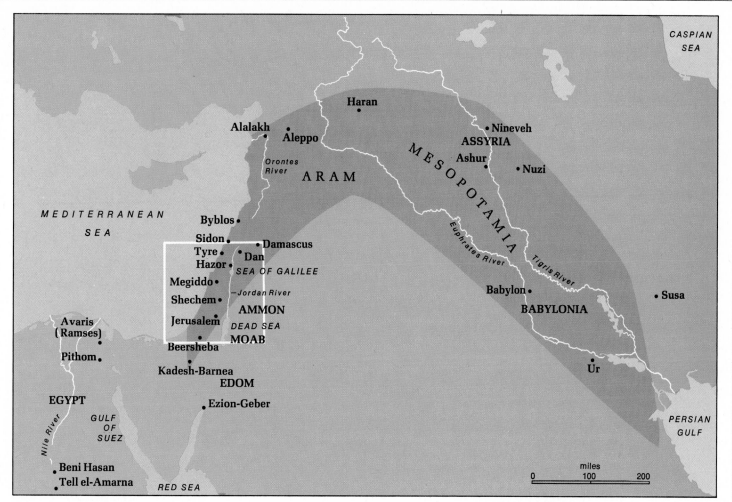

The map contains the following labels:

CASPIAN SEA

Haran

Alalakh • • Aleppo • Nineveh
ASSYRIA
Ashur • • Nuzi
Orontes River
ARAM
MESOPOTAMIA

MEDITERRANEAN SEA

Byblos •
Sidon •
Tyre • • Damascus
Hazor • • Dan
SEA OF GALILEE
Megiddo •
Shechem • — Jordan River
AMMON
Jerusalem • DEAD SEA
MOAB
Beersheba •

Euphrates River
Tigris River

Babylon •
BABYLONIA
• Susa

Avaris (Ramses) •
Pithom •
Kadesh-Barnea •
EDOM
Ezion-Geber •
EGYPT
GULF OF SUEZ
Nile River
Beni Hasan •
Tell el-Amarna •
RED SEA

Ur •

PERSIAN GULF

miles
0   100   200

The Fertile Crescent (green)—a broad, well-watered area stretching from the Mediterranean to the Persian Gulf—was the setting for the first centuries of the Israelites' history. In and around this productive land were numerous cities (bold type) and kingdoms (large type). Dominion over the small region that included Canaan (the boxed portion corresponding to the map opposite) was the coveted goal of many peoples.

Canaan, the narrow coastal strip between the Jordan River and the shore of the Mediterranean, was only 70 miles across at its widest part. In the 10th Century B.C. the Israelites established their monarchy there, assuming sway over many of the cities in the region and over some of the surrounding kingdoms.

The Cradle of Monotheism

The Israelites' wanderings over the span of more than 1,000 years took them through most of the ancient Near East. As the Bible chronicles their story, the family of the Israelites' patriarch Abraham left their home in the town of Ur sometime in the mid-Second Millennium B.C.; as nomads, they migrated westward over the Fertile Crescent to settle in Canaan. But Abraham's descendants traveled south to Egypt, where they were held in bondage until their escape, around 1225 B.C., under the leadership of Moses. As they headed back toward Canaan, the Israelites received the laws that were the basis of their monotheistic faith. Once resettled in Canaan, they established a monarchy that was to last into the Sixth Century B.C.

been written over a period of centuries in Canaan, after the Israelites settled there.

Nowadays most scholars, including the most religious, no longer regard the Bible as a story told chronologically. Instead, they view it as an accumulation of material, much of it repetitive, that was molded over many centuries—from both oral and written traditions—by many generations of storytellers who revised the stories endlessly in the telling, and by religious leaders who periodically brought the accounts up to date according to the biases of their times. Some of the Bible stories, representing a long history of recitations in village squares and around campfires in the wilderness, must have been set down in writing by the end of the Second Millennium B.C. But the written versions of the traditional stories were no more immune to the itch for revision than the oral versions had been. The Israelites were always looking for a better way to chronicle narratives already well known to them.

Nonetheless, ancient peoples were far less impatient with repetition of basic themes and plots than are modern readers or listeners; indeed, the very fact of repetition had its own incantatory power. Consider the five books once thought to have been written by Moses. The first, Genesis, tells the story of creation and traces the beginning of the Israelites' family tree to Abraham, Isaac and Jacob. The next four books—Exodus, Leviticus, Numbers and Deuteronomy—all recount the story of Moses and the Commandments, but they do so in different ways and with increasing elaborations—which to scholars give telltale indications that there was a series of several different contributors.

The reasoning that produces such conclusions derives from the archeological advances of the last hundred years. Excavations have uncovered the chronicles, letters, laws, hymns and prayers of other Near Eastern peoples whose paths the Israelites crossed. The new finds put traditional assumptions in bold relief—modifying some, clarifying others and bringing to light the circumstances in which these traditions took hold. Taken together, and seen in the light of the Bible as history, the discoveries draw an astonishing picture of religious, social, political, moral and intellectual development beginning about 4,000 years ago.

An example of this interpretive process involves a sequence in the Book of Chronicles. In the 18th year of the reign of King Josiah, according to the Chronicles, when the Temple of Jerusalem was being refurbished, the priests found parchment scrolls containing the law of Moses. Many of the laws were familiar to the priests, but the book itself was not. The high priest announced the discovery of something as ancient as Moses himself and promptly dispatched a scribe to tell the king. In the ensuing excitement Josiah summoned the inhabitants of Jerusalem, "the whole population, high and low. There he read them the whole book of the covenant discovered in the house of the Lord."

Modern scholars know, by comparing the concurrent records of neighboring peoples, that the 18th year of Josiah's reign was 622 B.C. And they believe that the scrolls that caused all this flurry formed the core of the book now called Deuteronomy. They also conclude that Deuteronomy cannot have been composed contemporaneously with the story it relates. They come to this conclusion by a roundabout process of reasoning, based on the fact that written

About 1500 B.C., when this stone portrait of a petty Syrian king was made, the pastoral forefathers of the Israelites—who were landless and kingless—were roving freely through small Near Eastern realms, trading cheese and wool for flour and metals. The robe on this 40-inch statue is densely inscribed with the biography of the monarch, who was named Idrimi.

words preserve, for the informed mind, certain evidences of the times in which they were written. The actual events involving Moses are thought to have occurred in the 13th Century B.C. But the vocabulary and viewpoint of Deuteronomy are largely those of the turn of the Seventh Century B.C.—less than 100 years before the time when Josiah's priests discovered and promulgated it.

It seems obvious that the priests were enthralled by what they had found because it struck them as divine writ, old as the beginnings of their belief. The fact that they already knew much of the contents bothered them not at all. Notwithstanding the sacredness they attached to the manuscript, they did not scruple to add new material to the book over the years and to revise parts of it to suit themselves; the Book of Deuteronomy as it has come down to us also bears their unmistakable stamp, just as it carries that of the original author.

Archeologists seeking to reconstruct the history of the Israelites look primarily to the region occupied today by Syria, Lebanon, Jordan and Israel. Much of this area was called the Land of Canaan in Biblical times; it was a long ribbon of territory reaching, at various points, 30 to 70 miles inland from the east coast of the Mediterranean Sea. From south to north it stretched approximately 250 miles—from the Sinai desert to the vicinity of Damascus. The Arabian and Syrian deserts bordered its eastern side and separated it from Mesopotamia, where the Akkadian, Babylonian, Assyrian and neo-Babylonian civilizations rose and fell between 2000 and 500 B.C. To the north lay the Hittites, Hurrians and other peoples whose cultures waxed and waned with varying ef-

Made in the Eighth Century B.C. and found in the coastal area inhabited by the Philistines, tiny clay cult figures of the fertility goddess Astarte—the largest six inches high—stand with hands symbolically placed under life-giving breasts. Israelite doctrine forbade possession of such idols, but influenced by ancient habits of worship, simple folk held onto them.

fects on the Israelites. Central to so many peoples and empires, Canaan was of concern to all of them; it was a trading route, a buffer zone, a battlefield, a campsite, a market, a political plum. It was also a seedbed of ideas, fostered by the mix of indigenous peoples and those passing through.

Inland, Canaan was a patchwork of rocky hills, grassy slopes, fertile plains and arid steppes. The Jordan River ran lengthwise down the land, and hundreds of lesser streams flowed from the hillsides —though some dried up entirely in summer. The country had a changeable climate that ranged from extreme heat in summer to damp chill in winter, and it suffered unpredictable afflictions of drought, locusts and earthquakes.

Nevertheless, Canaanite pastures were suitable for grazing sheep that provided wool, goats that yielded milk and cheese, and donkeys that carried the wool and other merchandise from city to city. And the soil nourished wheat, grapes, olives and figs, which provided the bread, wine, oil and fruit that people ate. Though the Land of Canaan was primarily a corridor for traders passing to and from the rich empires that lay beyond its borders, and a large oasis for the desert nomads who from time immemorial had looked upon the place as a land of milk and honey, the area nevertheless attracted a slow but ever-growing influx of permanent settlers.

They were as varied as the climate and the terrain —partly because they arrived at different times over long periods, and partly because the topographical arrangement of mountains, deserts and streams kept them in pockets of land that discouraged political or social homogeneity. However, for all their motley distinctions, the settlers were for the most part Semitic peoples—different branches of a common ethnic stock who spoke kindred dialects and shared a common primordial past as nomads.

As a desert people, the nomads lived off scattered oases, moving from one to another. But as families and tribes grew larger, they became too numerous for the oases to support them and their herds. Periodically, groups of them ventured out of the meager life of the desert. They went in all directions. In 2600 B.C. an Egyptian king wrote of "smiting the nomads of Asia"—meaning that the fringes of his empire were beset by raiding tribes. About 2400 B.C. their kin, far to the east, were populating northern Mesopotamia, where they were soon to found the Akkadian Dynasty, fuse with the already settled, non-Semitic Sumerians and then push south to form the Babylonian Empire. Throughout the next millennium, this process of dispersal, assimilation and redispersal continued, sometimes attended by warfare, but for the most part in peace.

As they chose places to settle and then stayed put, different branches of the same general Semitic family acquired different idiosyncrasies and new names. The Israelites, Amorites, Aramaeans, Moabites, Ammonites, Edomites and several others whose names occur throughout the Bible are from the same stock —though the Hittites, who also figure in the Bible, were unrelated, being of the Indo-European family. The Semites settled in various places—some founding cities, others establishing small kingdoms in Canaan and the adjacent regions.

Coming into Canaan in separate waves over more than a thousand years, the Semites went through stages of emergence from nomadic to agricultural and finally urban life. As nomads, they had traveled a

Plants Rooted in Scriptural Lore

In the days of the Israelites, the Near East blossomed with plant life whose descriptions enriched the texture of the Bible. In all, the Old Testament refers to some 100 different flowers, trees and vegetables, and though some are rare in the region today, botanists can confirm that the flora cited in the scriptures did indeed flourish there thousands of years ago. The fine engravings shown here, from early 19th Century A.D. botanies, illustrate four plants that thrived in Biblical times.

EXODUS 2: 2 AND 3

When she saw what a fine child he was, she hid him for three months, but she could conceal him no longer. So she got a rush basket for him, made it watertight with clay and tar, laid him in it, and put it among the reeds by the bank of the Nile.

Papyrus, or bulrush, grew in abundance along the banks of the lower Nile. Its stems, each topped by a large tuft, were used to make vessels like the one Moses' mother hid him in.

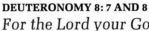

DEUTERONOMY 8: 7 AND 8

For the Lord your God is bringing you to a rich land, a land of streams, of springs and underground waters gushing out in hill and valley, a land of wheat and barley, of vines, fig-trees, and pomegranates, a land of olives, oil, and honey.

One of the promised blessings of the Holy Land, the pomegranate—a thick-skinned fruit whose name means "apple with seeds"—was widely cultivated in ancient times. The pulp contains compartments of juicy red seeds that were welcome refreshment for wanderers in the desert.

EXODUS 25: 10 AND 11

Make an Ark, a chest of acacia-wood, two and a half cubits long, one cubit and a half wide, and one cubit and a half high. Overlay it with pure gold both inside and out, and put a band of gold all round it.

Even in very dry places, such as the Sinai desert and the lands around the Dead Sea, acacias still thrive and bear delicate yellow blossoms. Because the wood of this thorny tree is close grained and hard, it has always been prized by cabinetmakers—hence its selection for the ark to house the covenant.

HOSEA 14: 4 AND 5

Of my own bounty I will love them; for my anger is turned away from them. I will be as dew to Israel that he may flower like the lily.

In the area that had been Canaan, scientists hunted in vain for physical traces of lilies—until 1925, when a crevice in Lebanon yielded one specimen. In early times the terrain—less arid than today—sustained lilies in profusion.

more or less fixed circuit in seasonal rotation, like migrating birds, going where grass was green, weather tolerable and food easily obtained. But eventually the migrants tended to take up part-time farming for a season; in a bountiful year some stayed on instead of moving along, and then found themselves farming permanently. Others, trading fleece and cheese for tools and adornments, embraced commerce and moved into cities, or formed cities of their own.

Canaan began sprouting settlements as early as 3000 B.C. After 2000 B.C. two strings of cities ran through Canaan, one on the coast, the other lying inland —forming a link between Egypt, Anatolia and Mesopotamia. Besides offering homes to erstwhile wanderers, the Canaanite cities were posts on the highways that ran between the great empires. They served as trading marts, storage depots, fortifications, caravan layovers and watering holes. Among the inland centers were Hebron, Jerusalem, Jericho, Shechem, Megiddo and Hazor—leading north to Damascus and Aleppo, where the road forked to go southeastward toward Mesopotamia and northward toward Anatolia. Along the coast, the second tier of cities—Ugarit, Byblos, Sidon and Tyre—linked up with the same route. In the course of the Second Millennium B.C., these coastal cities, besides sharing in the caravan trade, were to develop a rich sea trade with Egypt and with Cyprus, Crete and Mycenae.

With so many peoples crossing the same paths, and so much wealth in circulation through commerce, different interests were bound to clash; the Canaanite cities had to suffer the depredations of war even as they enjoyed the blessings of trade. Periodically, they came under the heel of one or another of the surrounding empires, which demanded tribute and installed provincial governors over large stretches of territory; these were sometimes the younger sons of the foreign ruling dynasties. The conquerors sent in standing armies or hired local mercenaries to keep conquests in line and adversaries at bay. Despite these assaults on their freedom, however, the Canaanite cities were too unruly to remain permanently under any single foreign power.

With respect to one another, the cities lived in sometimes friendly, sometimes quarrelsome, coexistence. Individual cities were generally ruled by a hereditary king, whose domain reached no farther than 20 miles in any direction beyond the city limits —a day's journey by caravan. A king generally shared his authority with a council made up of city elders: male members of old and wealthy families who joined the king in making decisions about military affairs, law and other matters.

Almost without exception the cities were perched on spring-watered hilltops. Even before the invention of the chariot—an instrument of surprise, with its military capabilities of speed and shock—settled peoples needed the heights as vantage points. From their hills they were able to spy across the plains and spot approaching trouble in ample time. The elevated locations were also platforms from which to hurl weapons upon unwelcome intruders. In times of drought and crop failure, marauders often came to help themselves to the spring water and the food that cities were known to keep in storage.

In time the permanent residents refined their defenses and built walls around most of the cities. Inside the walls craftsmen, merchants and scribes congregated in special quarters along narrow, wind-

Text continued on page 24

The Desert Nomads: for Centuries, a Harsh Life Style

On the northeast coast of the Sinai Peninsula, a seminomadic Bedouin tribe makes its summer encampment near a life-giving oasis.

These tribal Bedouin who dwell on the fringes of the Sinai desert follow a mode of life that, in many aspects, mirrors descriptions in the Book of Genesis of the Israelites' life style in Canaan after 2000 B.C.

The society is patriarchal; the women do all the household chores and tend the flocks. As has been true for 4,000 years, the seasons dictate the groups' movements: in the rainy time of year they pitch camp, with their flocks of sheep and goats, on the nearby mountains whose streams nourish grazing areas; from there the tribes move down to the thin pastures that surround the scattered oases.

Like other nomads, these Bedouin build shelters that are impermanent. The dwellings of the earliest Israelites were portable—small tents of hide or woven goat hair that they carried with them from pastureland to pastureland. These seminomadic Bedouin change their locations twice a year, as did ancestral Israelites; but their shelters are improvisations made of materials collected at the oasis: dead palm fronds laced to a structural framework of sticks.

Two members of the community of
Bedouin tend the herds of sheep and
goats whose well-being is the focus
of the tribe's day-to-day life. As
in patriarchal times, the animals are
slaughtered for meat only on special
occasions; they provide milk, and wool
and hair for weaving cloth. Surpluses
are sold or bartered to farmers
for grain and manufactured goods.

A Bedouin woman draws water from a stone-lined well fed
by the oasis' underground springs. Dates from the palm trees
are an important part of the tribe's diet. The metal container
and the robe protecting the woman against the scorching sun
resemble in design those used by the Israelites as early as
the patriarchal age, though the latter's vessels were ceramic.

ing streets. The houses inside the walls were built one against another, but as a city's population expanded, latecomers sometimes had to settle themselves just outside the wall.

Central to the life of the town was the spring. To it came men, women, children and animals to quench their thirst, and for household needs women brought pottery jugs to be filled and carried home again on their heads or shoulders. The same was largely true in cities around the eastern Mediterranean.

In the Book of Genesis, when Jacob, one of the Israelites' patriarchs, goes to the city of Haran in search of a bride, he first spies and falls in love with Rachel at a spring where she has brought her father's sheep to water. Archeologists have found many such springs in Canaan—and several that required elaborate engineering. One at Jerusalem and another at Megiddo stood outside the city walls instead of inside —probably because the settlement had shifted in the course of time. But in each instance the spring was reachable by a long underground tunnel and was hidden from view, presumably to prevent raiders from seizing the city's water supply.

By the end of the Second Millennium B.C. the inhabitants of Canaan no longer had to depend on a natural surface spring when settling a city; with improved drilling tools, they could cut through the limestone down to the water table. Another discovery—that lime plaster is waterproof—brought the invention of plaster-lined cisterns for collecting rain water. In most cities the cisterns, like the springs, were community property, though the kings and the elders in the rich city of Ugarit had such cisterns in the courtyards of their own households and had no need to go to the common font.

The city of Ugarit is one of the surprises of modern archeology. Unlike Jerusalem, Damascus and a number of others that have been continuously occupied from ancient times to the present, Ugarit was abandoned about 1200 B.C., after it was plundered and burned by invaders known to history only as the Sea Peoples, a horde that sailed in from the west. Other cities were to survive the Sea Peoples, but Ugarit, hidden under a 3,000-year accumulation of earth, lay forgotten until the ruins of the city were accidentally discovered by a farm boy in 1928. Subsequent excavation yielded a vast library of literature, much of which bears indirectly on the Israelites. It also turned up a palace with five courtyards, 11 staircases and 67 rooms—several with ivory-paneled walls—and among them at least one indoor bathroom.

Outside the Ugarit palace, the people lived modestly. Only the rich had courtyards. Most houses were one story high, made of brick and clay, sometimes supported with timber. But the size of a room was usually limited to the length of the tree trunks that supported the roof, and the rain that was welcome in the cisterns was a recurring problem on the rooftops: a Ugaritic text of the 14th Century B.C. notes that a good son was one who plastered the family roof against a rainy day.

Just as essential to the Canaanites' cities as houses were temples, which were considered to be the houses of the gods. The temples generally stood on sites where nomads had worshipped outdoors a thousand years before—and indeed some Canaanite worship continued outdoors even after the temples were built. The temples varied from city to city, but like most of those elsewhere throughout the Near East they generally consisted of three rooms, the innermost chamber being a holy-of-holies where the statue of a god was kept.

Like their neighbors the Egyptians, the Hittites and the Babylonians, the Canaanites of the Second Millennium B.C. worshipped hundreds of gods. These deities stood for a complex web of ideas that had been evolving as long as man himself. Evolution, of course, means change. In the course of this evolution, new gods often settled in with the old. But that did not mean that the old gods were displaced.

The polytheism of the Second Millennium B.C. was already such an old and rich accretion of human beliefs that pulling apart its separate components is a difficult task, and one that depends on a certain amount of guesswork. But some of the phases through which it passed can still be discerned, and they have a bearing on the history of the Israelites. For it was while moving about in a polytheistic world that the Israelites generated the monotheistic revolution that they handed on to modern man.

In man's earlier stages, when he lived hand in hand with nature, he saw deities in the elements on which his life depended—most notably earth and water. Ancient man also saw gods in the wild creatures with whom he shared the earth—the stag, the hawk, the fish, the lion, the bull; they were as mysterious as fire, and as intimately associated with his daily life. As soon as man could paint, he adorned altars and graves with such creatures.

As man's occupations became diversified and specialized, so did the spirits he worshipped. Herding peoples revered the ram, the goat and the cow. Farmers deified life-giving wheat and the intoxicating grape. But hunting, herding and farming peoples did not live in isolation; their paths crossed, they settled into villages together and their respective gods came to coexist just as people did.

Meanwhile, the time had come when man was no longer only herding and farming; he was developing the skills of pottery, metalworking, building in wood, stone and brick, carpentry, weaving, writing. The gods, who were already overseeing such occupations as herding and farming, quite naturally moved over to supervise the crafts and arts as well.

By the Fourth Millennium B.C., if not before, the gods had undergone a population explosion comparable to that of the human beings who worshipped them. They had also developed a social hierarchy to match their worshippers'. Just as a king ruled over human subjects, a god ruled over other gods. Kings rose and fell in power and importance; so did gods. A people whose fortunes prospered were thought to have an effective and powerful god watching over them, just as a nation required an effective and powerful king. When a conquering king took over a country, the god he worshipped usually came along and took a place in the local pantheon. A god was only as strong as the king who represented him on earth; in time a new god might come to prevail over older ones as chief of the pantheon.

This is a necessarily brief summary of a process that took place over several millennia. Along the way, some subtle shifts in viewpoint came about. One involved the roles of the godly spirits. Though many a god continued to reside in the water, in the bull, in the wheat and in the many other objects essential to man's livelihood, additional gods came to have special functions; they caused the rain to fall and the rivers to rise, the wheat to grow in abundance—or lie dormant in sterile earth—the flocks to increase and multiply, or to remain barren.

But man himself had a hand in causing the wheat to grow and the flocks to increase. And with man's increasing self-assertion over the world he lived in, another change in his view of divinity came about: more and more the gods took on human attributes, among them the emotions of love and hate, jealousy and generosity, anger and pleasure, grief and joy, gratitude and vengeance—even such minor, but potentially dangerous, feelings as annoyance.

Divine irritation supplies much of the dramatic momentum for the Epic of Gilgamesh, one of the oldest written narratives in the world. Based on the life of a hero called Gilgamesh, the saga is laced through with shifting ideas about the roles of humans and gods as man perceived them in the Third Millennium B.C., when the story was committed to writing in Mesopotamia. Several variations composed over hundreds of years throughout the Near East tell the tale of a cataclysmic flood; it is very much like the one recounted in the Book of Genesis, where the human hero is Noah, a deserving man who is saved from the disaster meted out to his sinful peers because his god selects him to build an ark in which he and his family can ride out the storm.

The Babylonian versions of this tale have many gods instead of one, and together the deities experience virtually every feeling known to man. According to one early variation, the cause of the flood was the human population, which grew so numerous, so rich and so rowdy, that Enlil, the sky god, could not sleep. He sent the people one plague after another, hoping to get some peace and quiet. But incorrigibly, the people kept up their racket. When all else had failed, Enlil sent the disastrous flood, intending to wipe out the annoyance altogether. He nearly succeeded, but Ishtar, the goddess of birth, set up a wail of despair and Ea, the god of wisdom, took aside his favorite human being, Atrahasis—like Noah, a worthy man. Ea told Atrahasis how to build a boat, gave him some animals and sent them all to safety. Thus, according to the epic, except for a combination of wise practicality and the unquenchable force of rebirth, the human race might have been done in forever by a fretful god who happened to be in need of a good night's sleep.

The humanization of the gods occurred all over the Near East, taking different forms. It reached one logical conclusion in Egypt, where the pharaoh was himself deemed to be a living god. It reached another in Mesopotamia, where the king was thought to be a sacred intermediary, appointed by the gods for the purpose of keeping order on earth.

The next step was taken by the Israelites—introducing to both the human and the divine spheres the concepts of morality and ethics, firmly linking law to the core of religious belief. In the Israelites' concept of the relationship of the regulating deity to mortal men, the obligation for abiding by the law was to rest on the human conscience. In the course of the Second and First millennia B.C., small groups of Israelites—a loose confederation of tribes linked by recognition of a common forebear and a common god —moved about among other peoples of the Near East. Assimilating here, modifying there, they drew on the cultural wealth they found around them and forged their own unique religious instrument.

Fragile Treasures from the Dead Sea Caves

Many Dead Sea Scrolls were discovered in the caves in these ancient cliffs above the Wadi Qumran, the dry stream bed at lower left.

Early in 1947 a young Bedouin, pursuing a stray goat in desolate Qumran, near the Dead Sea, stumbled upon a find that pushed back the frontiers of Israelite history by 1,000 years.

In one of the numerous caves that gape in the moonlike landscape, the Bedouin found a cache of ancient jars, one of which held leather scrolls covered with script. By autumn, the first scrolls had reached scholars in Jerusalem, who determined that they included the earliest-known copies of Old Testament texts. They had been set down around 100 B.C.—less than a century after the last of the Old Testament books was written—by members of an ascetic Jewish sect. Later probes of other caves around Qumran have recovered portions of all but one of the Old Testament books. Many of the finds are now in a special building at the Israel Museum in Jerusalem.

Prior to the discovery of the scrolls, the earliest Biblical manuscript in Hebrew dated to 900 A.D. There were discrepancies, significant to scholars, between that work and the many versions of the Old Testament that had been translated into Aramaic, Greek and Latin, then repeatedly copied and revised through the centuries. The scrolls have made it possible to analyze intensively, word by word, passage by passage, the variations among the ancient texts—and, in the process, to arrive at the most definitive Israelite record of their history ever assembled.

In Search of a Biblical Trove

During the decade after the first scrolls were found, the cliffs in the Dead Sea region were combed for more texts. Often following Bedouin treasure hunters, who sought the ancient writings for sale to antique buyers, archeologists probed more than 200 sites in the Qumran area alone; some were spacious caverns where they could work in comparative comfort, others hardly more than crevices. Of all the caves explored later, only 10 yielded the sought-after scrolls, most of which were badly deteriorated. But from the hundreds of fragments and the few relatively intact manuscripts found, scholars could cull portions of nearly all the books of the Old Testament.

Archeologists could hoist themselves up to caves like this one, in the face of an almost vertical 1,500-foot limestone cliff, only by mountaineering methods. Once inside, they plunged into dust some two feet deep and scoured it with brushes and tweezers in order to find the tiniest scroll fragments.

Known by its excavators as Cave IV, the relatively large cavern at right, about 24 feet deep, produced by far the richest finds. Bits of inscribed leather recovered here represented some 400 documents from the library of Qumran's early Jews, including parts of many Biblical and liturgical books.

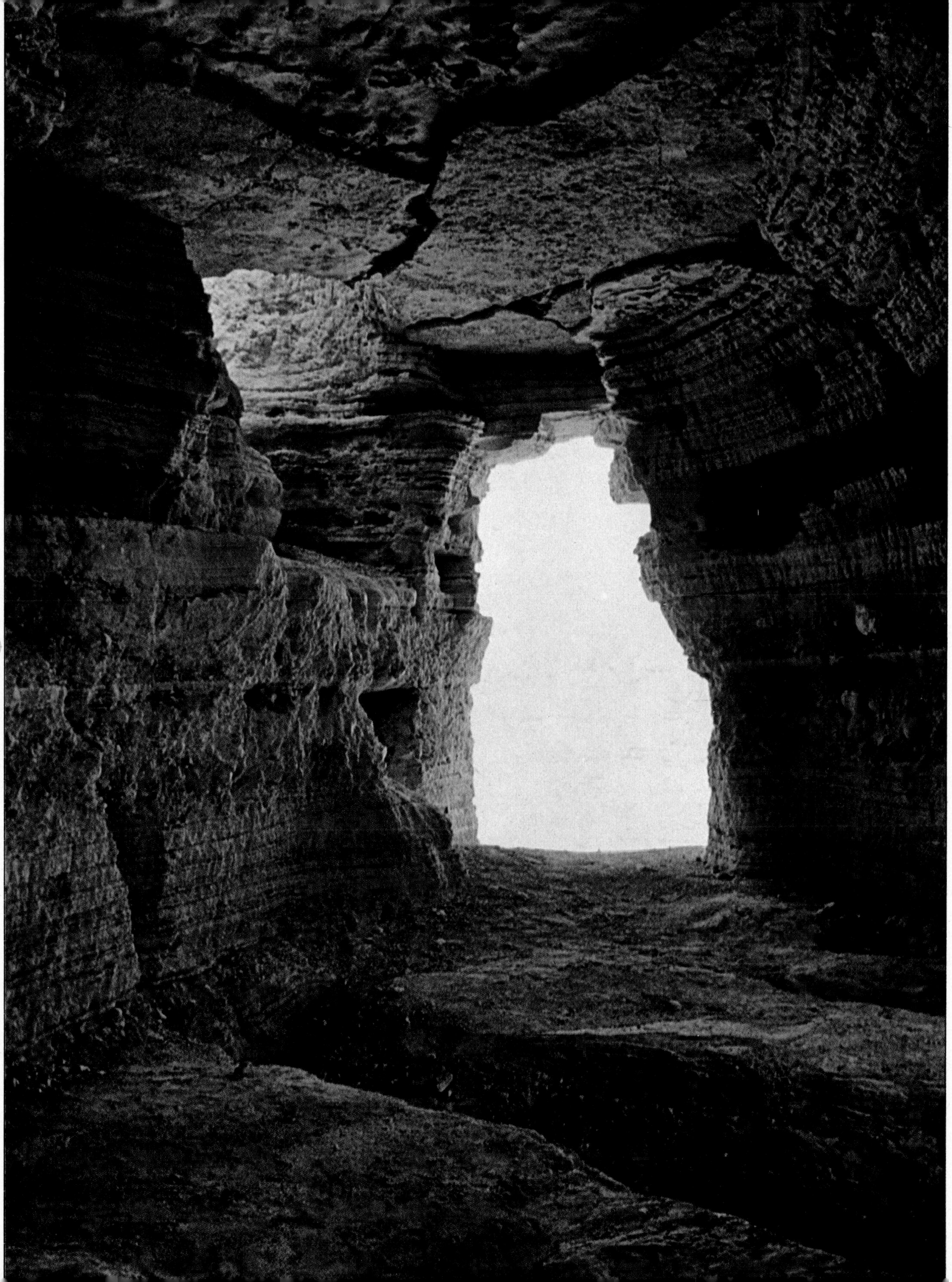

Unlocking 2,000-year-old Secrets

The covered jars in which the ancients had stored the precious scrolls served remarkably to prevent disintegration; nevertheless, 2,000 years in arid caverns took their toll. Since in many instances the leather had become bone dry and brittle, before the scrolls could be unrolled experts subjected them to a special humidifying process; then they could be flattened under glass. Fragments that were illegible because the leather had become so dark could be read only from photographs made under infrared light, which emphasizes subtle color differences. Finally, with all the problems of the texts' fragility solved, scholars could pore over their contents.

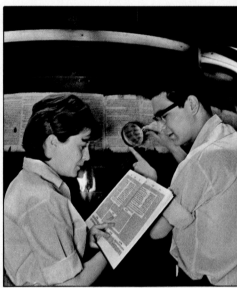

Students in Jerusalem read the text of the scroll containing the Book of Isaiah, which dates to the First Century B.C., against a text in Hebrew dating to 1525 A.D. Though the book must have been copied again and again in the intervening 1,600 years, the two texts hardly differ, indicating that as early as 100 B.C. the Israelites' descendants had standardized certain portions of their scriptures. The section of the Isaiah scroll opposite shows only minor evidence of the ravages of time.

These pottery jars, standing 18 and 25 inches high, contained some of the first Dead Sea Scrolls discovered. Within the terra-cotta vessels, the treasured leather documents were further protected with wrappings of linen.

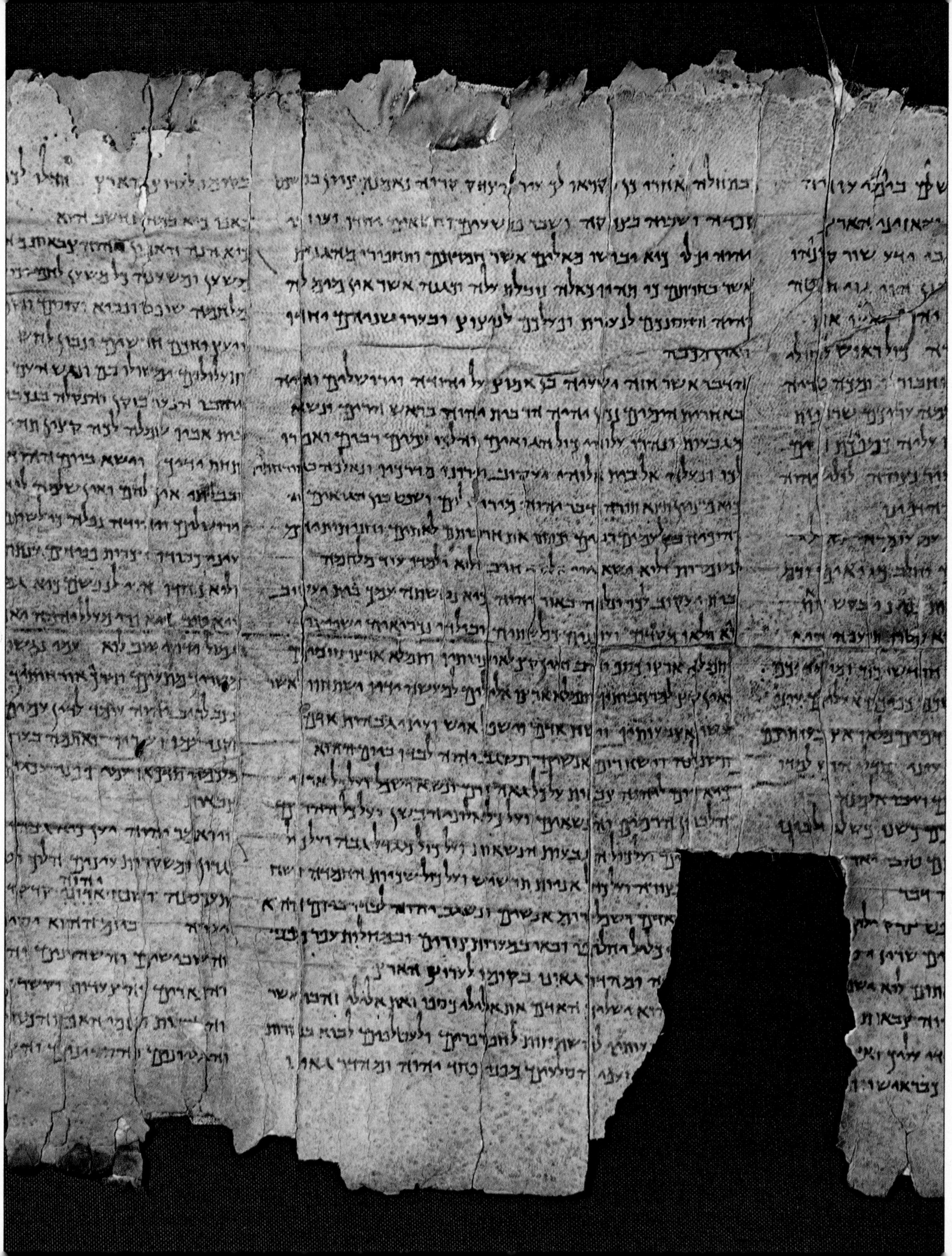

A Shrine for Ancient Texts

Striking in its design, the Shrine of the Book houses the Dead Sea Scrolls at the Israel Museum in Jerusalem. The sanctuary, on a hill over the city, is largely subterranean to evoke the mood of the caves where the scrolls were discovered. The part of the sacred building that lies aboveground—the tiled dome rising out of a moat (*below*)—symbolizes the covers of the jars that protected the texts for 20 centuries. At the sanctuary's heart (*opposite*) the scroll of the Book of Isaiah unrolls around a drum surmounted by a representation of the handle of a Torah, the traditional liturgical text still used in synagogues.

Flames flicker atop the black basalt wall at left, which stands beside the Shrine of the Book as a symbol of the Jews' long and difficult history. Visitors must pass through a tunnel to reach the principal chamber below the dome, whose solid surface is cooled in summer by jets of water from the moat.

Directly below the opening in the dome is the focal point of the sanctuary's interior—the 24-foot-long scroll of Isaiah. It consists of 17 leather sheets sewn together, on which are 54 columns of text. In cases around the walls of the memorial are fragments of other scrolls from the Dead Sea region.

Chapter Two: The Promise and the Covenant

For all peoples, religion embodies not only the divine figures who are the objects of veneration but also the flesh-and-blood teachers who carry the spiritual message to their fellow human beings, who nurture it, reinterpret it to fit new circumstances, defend it against erosion and hand it on to posterity. Among the Israelites, according to Biblical tradition, the first to fulfill these human roles were the patriarchs: Abraham, Isaac and Jacob; the three men—father, son and grandson—were the first to perceive and communicate with the god whom the Israelites, in time, came to worship to the exclusion of all others.

In the Book of Genesis, the god chose to appear before Abraham at a place called Haran and said: "Leave your own country, your kinsmen, and your father's house, and go to a country that I will show you. I will make you into a great nation." That nation, the later Israelites believed, was their confederation of 12 tribes. For the Israelites regarded their 12 tribes as the direct descendants of the 12 sons of Jacob, and they believed that Canaan was the country the Almighty had promised Abraham.

The Biblical account relates that Abraham did as he was bidden. He left Haran—a city on a plain east of the Euphrates River that was an outpost of Mesopotamian civilization—and traveled southwest. When he finally reached the city of Shechem in the Land of Canaan, his god appeared to him again,

In this detail of an 1800 B.C. wall painting from the palace at Mari on the Euphrates River in Mesopotamia, a bull—adorned with a white crescent and gilded horn tips—is led to ritual slaughter by a Semitic tribesman wearing characteristic dress. Animal sacrifices to the gods were basic to Near Eastern religions. When the Israelite patriarchs undertook to call upon their one god, they often did so after making a sacrifice.

saying: "I give this land to your descendants." So Abraham gratefully "built an altar there to the Lord who had appeared to him." In subsequent episodes of the Book of Genesis Abraham's son Isaac is said to have made similar covenants—commitments to worship "the god of his father" in exchange for divine favor—as did Isaac's son Jacob.

On that beginning the Israelites laid the cornerstone of their faith. They further came to believe that, as the direct descendants of Abraham, Isaac and Jacob, they themselves were bound to honor the original sacred covenant by worshipping "the god of their fathers." The whole body of monotheistic religion was later to rest on this principle of two-way trust between man and a supreme deity.

Abraham, Isaac and Jacob cannot themselves be strictly described as monotheists; the word generally connotes those who venerate one god to the exclusion of all others. The patriarchs' form of worship was not fundamentally at odds with the prevailing polytheism of their time. As the heirs of that rich tradition, they viewed their deity as a personal patron who would see them through the trials of life, much as the goddess of grain watched over the crops and the god of scribes looked after the craft of writing.

Nevertheless, the patriarchs stand at the origins of monotheism because they represent the first enunciation of the all-important principle that the faithful, and their descendants who worshipped the same god, constituted a family. By blood ties and in perpetuity, the members of that family were bound to the Almighty as they were to one another—with all the nuances of family trust, loyalty and security implicit in such a bond.

As archeologists now know, the god of the Israelites arose during the Second Millennium B.C. in a society held together by obedience to family rules. Such social matters as inheritance and marriage were overseen by the one patriarch of the extended family. So too were the spiritual matters that carry the main burden of the Biblical story of the patriarchs.

According to the account in Genesis, Abraham and his progeny remained in the Land of Canaan down to the fourth generation, except for periodic necessary excursions east and west toward Mesopotamia and Egypt. The narrative closes with Jacob's sons successfully settled in Egypt, where they had originally gone to escape a famine in Canaan. The account probably sums up the folk memory of the mass migrations of one or more branches of the Semitic tribes who shifted about the Near East throughout the Second Millennium B.C.

It is difficult to find archeological traces of any ancient nomadic people because of the nature of their life style. But if there has been no hard physical proof that the individual patriarchs, Abraham, Isaac and Jacob, were actual human beings, plenty of scholarly evidence does exist to support the conclusion that there is substantial historical truth in the patriarchal narrative. Discoveries of shrines and records—letters, legal codes and civil contracts—belonging to peoples who were contemporaries and neighbors reveal a great deal about the social structures, the manners and mores in Mesopotamia, Syria, Canaan and Egypt during the Second Millennium B.C.; and the story of the patriarchs as the Bible recounts it is filled with details that coincide with the archeological data.

It becomes increasingly possible to assume that the patriarchal roles parallel those of the ancient family chieftains. It is not at all clear, however, whether the Israelites they led were herders, moving their sizable flocks from pasture to pasture, and from time to time into the cities to sell their fleece and goat hair; or caravan traders who traveled the route between Mesopotamia and Egypt by way of the cities in Canaan.

Archeologists know that for a period of some 800 years, from about 2000 B.C. to about 1200 B.C., several Semitic families, or tribes, pursued both activities. Though scholars differ over tribal identities and disagree about details of chronology, they nevertheless generally agree that the patriarchal age began no earlier than 1950 B.C. and ended no later than 1300 B.C. Some experts believe the age lasted only a hundred years or so—enough to cover the three generations spanned in the Book of Genesis. Those who suppose that the patriarchal age lasted for the 650-year period suggest that the figures of Abraham, Isaac and Jacob came to represent different, and possibly quite widely separated, phases of the Israelites' ancestral history—eras that in time were telescoped, by those who transmitted the oral tradition, into three generations. The stories ascribed to the patriarchs might even represent different branches of the Semitic family tree, whose several memories eventually merged in a common ethnic history.

Modern scholars are still in the process of piecing together a more complete, if nonetheless impressionistic, picture of the early Israelites based on close study of the Bible in relation to what is known of contemporary cultures. For example, the Bible is filled with references to one important branch of the large and ever-moving Semitic family. Called Amorites, the members of that line are generally seen as the natural enemies of the patriarchs and of their descendants. The fact is that they were probably kin—just different waves of the same migrations. Whether they were related or not, the Amorites inhabited parts of Canaan, the Israelites' chosen land, and seem to have led similar lives. Consequently, discoveries about the former shed light on the latter.

The records of other peoples of the Near East early in the Second Millennium B.C. are full of references to the Amorites. Most of the comments are uncomplimentary, but in the process of being critical they add substantially to the picture of their times. The word *Amurru,* whence the English name of the group derives, meant "west" in the Akkadian language, which was the written lingua franca throughout the Near East at that time. *Amurru* referred to the vast, arid region in which lie the modern Arabian and Syrian deserts, where the Amorites originated; it lay between Mesopotamia and the green hills and rushing streams of the Land of Canaan.

The Akkadians were also Semites and therefore distant kin to the Amorites. Nevertheless, they too reviled those nomads who lived in the west as foreigners who "do not know any crops," and scorned the chief god of the Amorites as "one who lives in a tent, exposed to wind and rain, who digs truffles at the foot of the mountain, who does not bend a knee, who eats raw foods, who has no home during his lifetime, and no tomb at his death."

The Egyptians called these nomads sand-crossers and Asiatics. Then, as now, people who were deemed alien and backward became handy targets for scorn and derision.

There were exceptions to this general hostility, which in the process of being recorded preserved important insights into Amorite manners and attitudes.

Toward those whom they knew and trusted, the nomads were lavish with their hospitality, and generated appropriate gratitude in return. An Egyptian court official named Sinuhe, who left his homeland during a change of kings about 1960 B.C. and started toward Syria, paid homage to this generosity in an account of his desert journey. He had fully expected trouble en route, but at one stop along the way ran into a pleasant surprise.

"I was parched, and my throat was dusty," he wrote. "This is the taste of death! But then I lifted up my heart and collected myself, for I had heard the sound of the lowing of cattle, and I spied the Asiatics. The chief among them, who had been in Egypt, recognized me. Then he gave me water while he boiled milk for me." And Sinuhe acknowledged thankfully that "what they did for me was good."

The land between Mesopotamia and Egypt was populated with Semitic tribes or family groups like the one Sinuhe encountered. Each lived under the leadership of its own patriarchal head. These chieftains controlled grazing and watering rights over certain stretches of land; they had large bands of retainers and owned sizable herds of sheep and goats.

For all their vaunted hatred of the Amorites, then, the patriarchs of Canaan in many respects seem to have resembled them, judging by Sinuhe's general description. The Bible indicates that Abraham, Isaac and Jacob—as each inherited the role of patriarch —held a territory. The stories about them illustrate the customs for honoring such territoriality:

On Jacob's return to Canaan after a sojourn in Haran, he must pass through the country of Edom, where there is a district ruled by his brother Esau with whom he has had a falling-out over their inher-

A shepherd and his flock pass the ruins of the huge ziggurat, or temple, at Ur, first constructed in the 23rd Century B.C. In the foreground are the foundations of the city's residential and commercial center, composed around a maze of lanes linking dwellings, workshops, schools and much smaller places of worship. According to the Old Testament, Ur was the patriarchs' place of origin; from here Terah, accompanied by his son Abraham, began his migration to Haran, where he was to die. It was from Haran that Abraham, having received the divine mandate, set off for Canaan.

itance. En route, messengers bring Jacob a warning: "We met your brother Esau already on his way to meet you with 400 men." Fearful, Jacob decides to soften Esau's heart with a show of generosity.

The Bible again, still speaking of Jacob: "As a present for his brother Esau, he chose from the herds he had with him 200 she-goats, 20 he-goats, 200 ewes and 20 rams, 30 milk camels with their young, 40 cows and 10 young bulls, 20 she-asses and 10 he-asses. He put each herd separately into the care of a servant," and sent them on ahead.

Then follows a scene in which Jacob and Esau emotionally greet each other with bows and embraces. Esau, not to be outdone in elaborate courtesy, declines to take the proffered herds and sends his brother on his way, offering some of his own men as escorts through the territory he dominates.

Because of such tales as these, and because of the pastoral imagery and insights into life style that run throughout the Book of Genesis, the patriarchs have traditionally been thought of as nomadic herders, as indeed they may have been. But there were other men who constantly shuttled between Mesopotamia and Egypt during the patriarchal age. They were the caravaners, and what modern research has confirmed about them is not in substantial conflict with the Biblical accounts. On that basis, some scholars now suggest that Abraham could have been the wealthy and sophisticated chief of a caravan that plied the trade routes running through the Land of Canaan.

Caravan leaders arranged the expeditions that transported the luxuries and the necessities of life from one end of the civilized world to the other. This traffic was the big business of the Second Millennium B.C., engaging people of many occupations. Artisans

Turkish shepherds guide their donkeys and sheep on a dusty trail to water holes near a tower on the outskirts of the village of Haran. It was here, according to tradition, that Abraham, aged 74, was told by his god to begin the quest for the Holy Land. So charged, Abraham gathered up his meager possessions and, with his wife Sarah and his nephew Lot, started south.

in the major cities used raw materials brought from afar to manufacture the goods that were destined for dispatch and consumption abroad. From mines in Anatolia caravans brought silver; from the island of Bahrain in the Persian Gulf ships carried copper and precious stones; from Afghanistan came lapis lazuli. Craftsmen everywhere in the Near East made all these into jewelery and statues of the gods. The ivory that adorned the houses of Ugaritic nobles originated in Nubia, on the upper Nile. Lebanon exported cedar, which the Egyptians used to build ships, and from which they extracted rosin to use for embalming mummies. Syria produced musical instruments: the lute and the flute. The oases in the Arabian Desert traded in incense. And Egypt manufactured papyrus, shipped east in scrolls that were later used to record the Bible.

The men who ran the caravans were sometimes agents of the kings; in the large empires, business was a monopoly of the state. But some caravaners were private entrepreneurs; and this was particularly true in Canaan, which lacked a centralized government to monopolize trade, but lay athwart the roads by which trade moved and contained many cities on which commerce fed. Such a region, far from the seats of imperial power and yet essential to international dealings, was congenial to men of an independent frame of mind, who could operate there on their own and negotiate with clients from points all along the line.

Caravaners had frequent dealings with the cities, yet always remained apart from them. Like the nomads, the caravaners lived intimately with nature, pitching tents outdoors whenever they needed temporary shelter. En route, they trafficked with the herders who bred the donkeys they needed to carry their cargoes, and who sold them milk and fleece for trade goods; the caravaners also traded with farmers who produced food grains and olive oil for cooking. Sometimes they had to negotiate with the unsettled desert nomads for the security of their caravans. In a cache of clay tablets found on the site of Tell el-Amarna, the 14th Century B.C. capital of Egypt, was a letter from the king of the Canaanite city of Hazor, who wrote the pharaoh: "My caravan has escaped, it is intact"—a sure sign that safe passage through the nomads' territory was a constant subject of worry.

There was good reason for concern. The caravans, which could be very large, often had a great deal of wealth riding with them. One 19th Century B.C. Egyptian inscription in cuneiform, found in Mesopotamia, describes a caravan consisting of 600 donkeys; since the donkeys carried more than 150 pounds apiece, more than 90,000 pounds of supplies and merchandise apparently were being transported on just that one expedition.

The clay tablets go on to reveal much additional minutiae—all contributing to the painstaking scholarly reconstructions of the times. For example, the donkeys were black and strong. They traveled over winding, rocky paths, covering from 20 to 25 miles a day. They carried food to sustain the human and animal members of the party during 10-day stretches through the uninhabited parts of the desert. The expedition required an attendant for every five donkeys, so that a caravan of 600 donkeys must have had some 120 attendants.

Perhaps the most important reason cited by scholars to support the theory that Abraham might have been a caravan leader rather than a chief of herders

Reconstructing Life in Early Jericho

In 1955 archeologists excavating tombs near ancient Jericho, in Israel, discovered the extraordinary remains of a family that had been ravaged by a plague some 3,500 years ago and of household effects buried with them. Mysteriously, some of the perishable materials—including wood, rush baskets and the remnants of food—were impressively well preserved due, some scientists theorized, to ambient gases trapped inside the tomb that stayed decay.

Based on the find as it was first seen at right, experts were able to reconstruct the domestic scene shown below it. The time is 1600 B.C. The dwelling is of mud brick. The occupants are one man, two women and three children.

Their life style was typical of the period when the Israelite patriarchs were wandering in Canaan.

Among the objects inside the tomb were reed baskets and wooden furniture. A long table bore traces of a mutton joint and fruit, and an ivory-inlaid box. Scattered throughout were remnants of pottery plates and urns.

Working from the unusually complete and relatively intact find, an archeologist-artist re-created a mealtime scene in a Jericho household. All the artifacts seen in the drawing were reconstructed from the evidence of fragments in the tomb. The bed (foreground)—string laced onto a wooden frame—was the rarest item.

is geographic; the route between Ur, the Mesopotamian city in which he is supposed to have been born, and Haran, the city he is said to have left for Canaan, was a major axis of Mesopotamian trade. The very name Haran in Akkadian may mean "caravan station." Haran lay on a flat river plain that was suitable for grazing; it therefore attracted nomads from the desert. But it was also a center for trade coming from Anatolia in the north and from Syria, Canaan and Egypt in the southwest.

Biblical tradition also assigns to Abraham a brother named Haran; and figures of lore often bear names synonymous with their places of origin, their occupations, or both. Even more compelling is the discovery that all the sites where Abraham is said to have worshipped in the Promised Land—Shechem, Bethel, Hebron and Beersheba—were way stations on the caravan route through Canaan.

At these sites the patriarchs—or their contemporaries among the Canaanites—left some evidence of their activities. In 1960 members of an archeological expedition at Bethel, digging in search of the temple of Jeroboam, an Israelite king who lived in the 10th Century B.C., failed to find what they were looking for. Instead, however, the diggers found something else of extraordinary interest to students of the patriarchal period. Several layers below the surface of the soil the team uncovered the ruins of a structure they identified as a temple, which had evidently been in use for a long time, beginning about the 19th Century B.C. In the temple were animal bones and flints of the sort used in slaughtering animals and scraping skins—sure signs that animal sacrifice had taken place in the temple. Then, digging beneath the temple's foundations, at a level that dates to about 3000 B.C., the archeologists found a flat table-like stone bearing what appeared to be prehistoric bloodstains that had dripped down its sides. The stone at Bethel was doubtless an outdoor altar of the sort that Abraham, Isaac and Jacob are said to have worshipped at throughout the Biblical narrative.

The importance of Bethel in the Israelites' history is reinforced by the fact that it is the scene of one of the most famous patriarchal tales, Jacob's dream of a heavenly ladder—a story that fascinates scholars intent on determining its significance.

The Bible tells us that, en route to Haran from Canaan, Jacob lay down one night to sleep. He "dreamed that he saw a ladder which rested on the ground with its top reaching to heaven: and the angels of God were going up and down on it." Archeologists theorize that the ladder represents the long flights of steps that conventionally led up the sides of Mesopotamian temple towers. They speculate further that the angels ascending and descending the ladder might well translate as the priests of the temple, who made ritual processions up those steps in the belief that the local deity descended from the heavens to meet them at the top of the tower. Acceptance of this interpretation of Jacob's ladder would add several links to the chain of evidence connecting the Israelite patriarchs with Mesopotamia.

One of the patriarchs' major concerns was arranging marriages for the children to suit the family's interests, and the most effective partners were to be found on ancestral home grounds. According to Genesis, after Abraham had moved to the Land of Canaan, he sent a servant to Haran, where his kin remained, to fetch a suitable wife for his son Isaac. The servant brought back Rebecca, for whose hand he had to negotiate with the head of her own family.

When Isaac's son Jacob reached marriageable age, he in turn followed the tradition; at his father's bidding he duly went to Haran, the land of his grandfather, to fetch a suitable wife. He returned with two—Rachel and Leah, the daughters of his maternal uncle, Laban—along with two concubines, the ladies' maids of Rachel and Leah.

The story that surrounds this marital journey is full of implicit and explicit insights into the life of the Israelites' forebears. Perhaps the most compelling elements of the story involve ancient attitudes toward marriage, property and religious values—attitudes that are all intertwined.

To begin with, Jacob is not allowed to march home immediately with his womenfolk; to win them he must put in many long years of service to Laban. Meantime, he is allowed to marry Rachel and Leah, and to father their children. In his own good time, Laban rewards Jacob for his service with a herd of

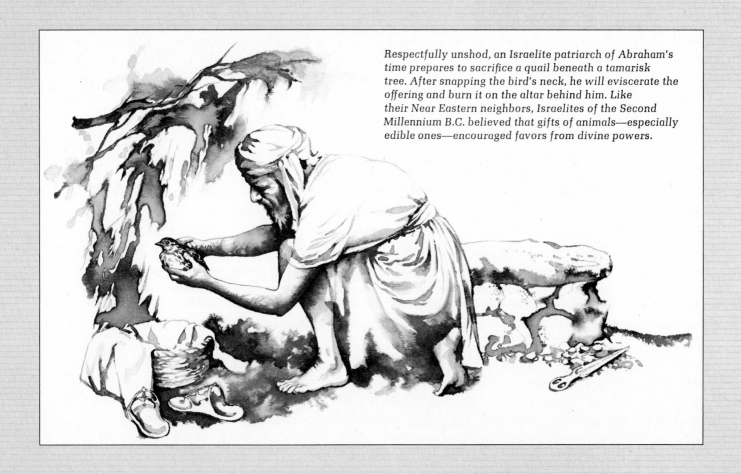

Respectfully unshod, an Israelite patriarch of Abraham's time prepares to sacrifice a quail beneath a tamarisk tree. After snapping the bird's neck, he will eviscerate the offering and burn it on the altar behind him. Like their Near Eastern neighbors, Israelites of the Second Millennium B.C. believed that gifts of animals—especially edible ones—encouraged favors from divine powers.

several hundred spotted goats and black sheep, along with cattle, camels and donkeys. Then, having acquired all these animals, Jacob packs up, gathers his women and his herds, and departs without a word to Laban, heading home to Canaan—a journey of more than 350 miles in a straight line, but far longer over winding, hilly rock-strewn paths.

The Bible explains that Jacob takes this unannounced leave because he fears that otherwise the untrustworthy Laban will find some way of preventing his departure. The account goes on to say, however, that when Jacob has traveled only partway, Laban overtakes the party, full of reproaches for Jacob: "What have you done?" Laban exclaims. "Why did you slip away secretly without telling me? I would have set you on your way with songs and the music of tambourines and harps. You did not even let me kiss my daughters and their children."

All this is bad enough, but Laban saves his bombshell for last: "Why did you steal my gods?" He is referring to figurines representing his ancestral deities. They are so important that their loss drives him to pursue Jacob in an attempt to recover them.

Jacob protests his genuine innocence and invites Laban to have a look around. Laban searches high and low throughout the camp without success. He enters a tent where he finds Rachel seated on a pile of baggage, and she begs her father to excuse her from rising to greet him, pleading demurely that she is unwell with "the common lot of woman." Rachel is hiding the idols under her skirts; and so, though Laban searches the tent, he fails to find them. He apologizes to Jacob, the two erect a stone to mark their reconciliation, slaughter one of their herd and feast upon it, and Laban goes home to Haran while Jacob

Absorbed in private thoughts, a worshipper pours a libation of wine over an altar beside a memorial pillar. Among the Israelites, dedication of wine to their god was a joyful expression of gratitude in both public and personal affairs. A priest might make such an offering in thanks for his people's victory in a military campaign or for a good harvest that ended a period of famine. Or a similar gift might be presented by a father when a sick child became well or when a healthy infant was born.

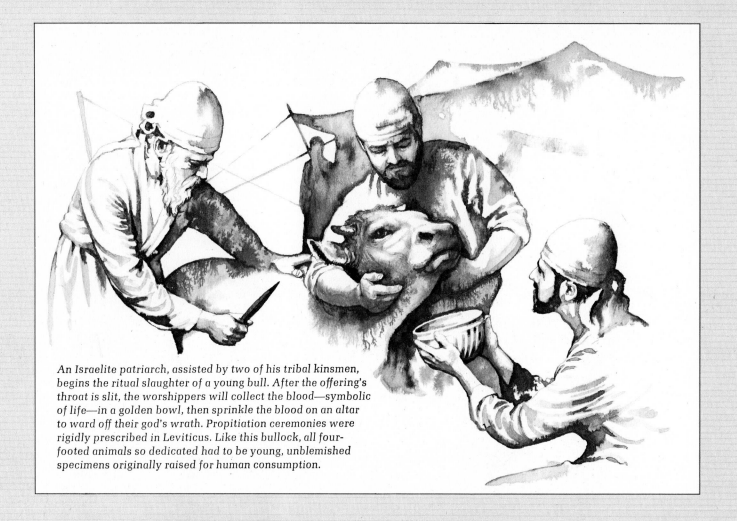

An Israelite patriarch, assisted by two of his tribal kinsmen, begins the ritual slaughter of a young bull. After the offering's throat is slit, the worshippers will collect the blood—symbolic of life—in a golden bowl, then sprinkle the blood on an altar to ward off their god's wrath. Propitiation ceremonies were rigidly prescribed in Leviticus. Like this bullock, all four-footed animals so dedicated had to be young, unblemished specimens originally raised for human consumption.

and his entourage resume their journey westward.

The Bible has nothing more to say about this episode. But it worried scholars and theologians for years; Rachel apparently goes unpunished for sins encompassing theft, sacrilege and falsehood.

Some of the historical and moral implications underlying the story came to light in a series of excavations begun in 1925 at the Mesopotamian city of Nuzi, which lay some 250 miles southeast of Haran. Among the finds at Nuzi were 15th Century B.C. tablets documenting marriage contracts. They show that in Nuzi, no less than among the Biblical patriarchs, marriage conventionally took place within existing family units; and property was expected to stay within the family. For the man who had no sons, the law provided a loophole: he could legally designate an heir to his property. Such an heir was generally someone who had worked as overseer of the man's property, as Jacob had toiled for Laban.

One Nuzi tablet—signed by five witnesses in addition to the scribe, and thus reflecting the solemnity this society attached to a contract—records an arrangement between a man named Nashwi and another named Wullu, who married Nashwi's daughter. It reads in part: "As long as Nashwi is alive, Wullu shall provide food and clothing." In effect that is what Jacob did in managing Laban's property. "If Nashwi has a son of his own," the tablet continues, "he shall divide the estate equally with Wullu, but the son of Nashwi shall take the gods of Nashwi."

The meaning of this contract is straightforward. Of all the property a man of Nuzi might have to settle on his heirs, none ranked so high in importance as his household gods, the divine patrons who were be-

In a later phase of the ceremony opposite, a patriarch sets pieces of meat to char in a wood fire on a stone altar. The bullock's head and suet will be added next. In the background two assistants—following the scripture's command—wash the animal's dismembered legs and entrails before adding them to the altar fire. The scent of cooking meat was intended to appeal to the deity and encourage his blessing, for the early Israelites believed that their god had desires similar to man's.

lieved to oversee his earthly welfare. The figurines that symbolized such divine patrons—which Rachel had made off with—were obviously thought to have magical powers as talismen. They were also part of a man's estate, something he bequeathed to his son, if he had one, or to a legally designated heir.

Seen against the background of the Nuzi tablets, the Jacob-Laban-Rachel story assumes a historical dimension—the shape of an account describing an actual sequence of events. Since the Bible does not identify any living sons of Laban at the time Jacob agreed to stay with him, Jacob can be seen as the kind of legal heir mentioned in the Nuzi tablets.

Moreover, the Bible does say that Rachel and Leah were angry at their father for not making *them* his heirs in the absence of such a son. Under the circumstances what could have been more plausible than Rachel's theft of the paternal gods? First, they were the most valuable of her father's possessions. Second, her father had not willed them either to her or to Jacob, the legal substitute heir who was, as well, her husband. Third, she had a perfect opportunity to lay hands on the gods in secrecy, since she knew Jacob intended to depart without informing Laban.

Extrapolating from such interpretations, scholars have been able to throw some revealing light on the historical origin of the god of Abraham—the focal point of the whole Book of Genesis. In bringing along a patron god as he left Haran for Canaan, Abraham was clearly following well-established, common practice. So were his son and grandson, who after his time venerated the god of their fathers and looked upon that god, and the blessings believed to emanate from him, as part of their inheritance, both literally and figuratively. But they modified that inheritance to fit new needs when they found themselves in different circumstances in lands far away, and absorbed new ideas as they settled in Canaan.

One of these acquired concepts may have been the very name of the god they worshipped. After the patriarchs' time the name of the god commonly associated with the Israelites was Yahweh. That name does occur a number of times in Genesis, but it was doubtless edited into the later written versions of this oft-repeated tale, and it does not come to predominate as the name for the deity until subsequent books of the Bible. The patriarchs themselves called the god they worshipped by other names, chiefly combinations of the word El.

In the Semitic languages El was a generic name for "god" or "deity," and El was also the name of the chief of the pantheon in Canaan. Often the patriarchs put that name in combination with another to suggest the divine attributes upon which they were calling at a given moment. Among these were El Shaddai, which may have meant God of the Mountain; El Elyon, possibly meaning Exalted One; El Olam, meaning God of Eternity or Everlasting One. In later generations, when the Israelites came to worship their god under the name of Yahweh (the precise meaning of which is lost), the term El as a name for "god" survived only in the old narrative about the patriarchs and in some literary forms, such as the Psalms. In much the same way, the obsolete "thee" and "thou" survive in modern liturgical usage and in poetry, although the words long ago dropped out of spoken English.

But the name El also survived in a subtle way, embedded in the names of several places and people that figure in the Biblical stories. One such place is Bethel: the name of one of the shrines where the Israelites worshipped, it means "house of God." Israel is the name the descendants of Jacob took upon themselves. It derived from an incident attributed to Jacob. According to Genesis, on Jacob's return to Canaan after the long stay in Haran, the deity appeared to him and said: "Your name shall no longer be Jacob, but Israel"—a combination of the name El with a Semitic word that means "striving." As a result of that episode, Jacob's progeny became the Children of Israel—or the Israelites.

Beyond providing the name of the god El and the story that describes the forging of the covenant with him, Genesis tells us little of what the patriarchs believed as such. But that is not surprising; in most religions formal credos are the work of later men. The early Biblical narratives simply say of the patriarchs that they were visited by visions of their god, who usually appeared in human form, and that they repeated such rituals as erecting altars, pouring oil on them, and slaughtering calves, lambs, kids and turtledoves. The patriarchs performed such sacrificial acts as a form of prayer: a gift offered up spontaneously in the hope of pleasing their god, or of securing a favor for protection.

In terms of formal religious practice that was about all. There were no prescribed times for worship. The observances were family affairs. There were no mass gatherings of the kind that took place at the temples of Egypt and Mesopotamia, where large companies of priests conducted rituals according to set formulas, and the public at large could only be spectators —and then only part of the time.

Yet, despite the simplicity and independence of the patriarchs' ways, there is no evidence that they were

at odds with the established local priesthood in Canaan. Neither was the faith of Abraham, Isaac and Jacob a source of trouble with the Canaanite population as a whole; bitter fights erupted from time to time, but the disputes arose only over circumstances threatening to family honor. Indeed, the patriarchs used established Canaanite holy sites for their own worship, which suggests that they coexisted agreeably with their neighbors, who were already settled in the many city-states of Canaan.

In character the god the Israelites worshipped seems to have been—like the patriarchs themselves—the figure of a stern father. He was less forbidding than the storm god who headed many Mesopotamian and Anatolian pantheons, and less capricious than the fertility gods of the same regions, who might cause the soil to dry up and the flocks to go barren for unpredictable and inexplicable reasons.

But in his paternal concern for the welfare of his family, the patriarchs' god was authoritarian in administering the rules by which the family was to hold together. He required strict obedience, and he gave or withheld largess—in the forms of prosperity and numerous descendants—as his demands were met.

One chapter of Genesis recounts that the god commanded Abraham to slay his son Isaac, then eight years old, but stayed Abraham's hand at the last mo-

ment and asked him to slaughter a ram instead. Religious interpretation explains the episode as a test of Abraham's faith. But some scholars see the story as evidence that human sacrifice as a religious practice was not beyond the patriarchs' acceptance. It is known that the Canaanites of the Second Millennium B.C. did follow the custom (although it apparently was waning), because excavations at a shrine near the city of Gezer have yielded clay jars containing the charred bones of babies.

Thus the story of the patriarchs as recorded in Genesis introduces many of the major elements of monotheism: the idea of a covenant between man and a personal god; the image of a god watching over the human community as a father watches over his family—providing, rebuking, rewarding; and the concept that every man could be his own priest.

Two elements later considered basic to monotheism were altogether missing. One was the stipulation that only one god might be worshipped; the other was the belief that no other gods existed. The seed of the first of those two ideas was to germinate in the next phase of the Israelites' history. Its flowering was to take place after a long stay in Egypt where, according to Biblical tradition, the Israelites had gone in search of grain during a famine in Canaan; from Egypt the descendants of Jacob were to be led out of slavery by Moses—hero, leader and lawgiver.

Chapter Three: Exodus and Commandments

The turning point in the history of the Israelites was reached not in the Promised Land, but during the desert journey to Canaan from Egypt where, according to Biblical tradition, they had been enslaved for generations. The Exodus itself, under the inspiration and leadership of Moses, signaled the Israelites' deliverance from oppression by foreign masters, a pivotal miracle wrought, they believed, by the god of their fathers. At some stage of the long trip across the dry wilderness leading to the Promised Land came the formulation of the Ten Commandments, the rigid code that created a permanent moral and ethical foundation for their religion.

More than 3,000 years later, the thrust of the Commandments survives as the basic force of Western civilization. Introducing the most famous prohibitions in all recorded history—the proclamations against murder, adultery and theft, among other transgressions—the Commandments begin: "I am the Lord your God who brought you out of the land of Egypt, out of the land of slavery. You shall have no other god to set against me."

That First Commandment established the Israelites' god—by this time called Yahweh—as an all-powerful being, capable alone of directing the entire course of human events; and the nine commandments that followed linked the Israelites' faithful worship of Yahweh to the principle that their religion demand-

ed justice in their dealings with their fellow men.

No archeologist has been able to trace the precise route of the Exodus, or to locate the sites of the major events of that journey as they are reported in the Bible. But modern scholarship holds that the lore of the flight and of the episodes that followed is basically true and probably occurred toward the end of the 13th Century B.C. somewhere on the Sinai Peninsula or perhaps in the Arabian Desert.

For all the factual uncertainties generated by the process of inquiry and by apparent errors of detail, there is no question that the Israelites' acceptance of the tradition dealing with the years in the wilderness was fundamental in fusing the separate tribes into a religious, political and historical unit. Their common god provided them with a national identity, a common way of worship, a common code of ethics, and a common goal: the Promised Land. The narrative brought to a new phase the already growing concept of monotheism; the First Commandment, while not explicitly denying the existence of plural gods, set the one god who was claimed as the source of all the Commandments above and beyond the contemporary pantheons of the Near East. And, most important, the new interpretation the Israelites put on human life, and the means they found for coping with their lives —drawn from the new codes of law—raised their religion above the limitations of a tribal cult. In that revolutionary process the Israelites' faith achieved the capacity to attract peoples beyond the bounds of their ethnic family and of the land they lived on.

The Biblical account of this next phase of the Israelites' history is told in the books of Exodus, Leviticus, Numbers and Deuteronomy, taking up the tale where Genesis leaves off. The sons of the pa-

Painted in the Third Century A.D., this fresco, more than four feet high, dramatizes a traditional view of Moses' God-given powers. Miraculously creating a well in the desert, he provides water for 12 tribesmen who, exhausted by the flight from Egypt, had lost confidence that he would save them. The work was discovered on the wall of a synagogue in Dura-Europos, an ancient city on the Euphrates River in Syria.

triarch Jacob, who was renamed Israel, are settled in Egypt, where they have gone to escape a disastrous famine in Canaan. The Egyptians enslave their descendants, who eventually depart from Egypt, and receive the Ten Commandments from Yahweh—as well as, in time, an elaborate corpus of other laws by which to live. They ultimately arrive, after a trouble-filled journey through the desert wilderness, at the threshold of the Land of Canaan. At the close of these four books, the 12 tribes stand assembled on the hills overlooking the Jordan Valley, ready to move in and settle down on the land promised their forefathers.

The human hero in all the stories that fill this sequence is Moses, reputedly a great-grandson of the patriarch Jacob's son Levi. According to the legends surrounding his life, Moses was born in Egypt at a time when the pharaoh, alarmed by the rate at which the Israelite population was increasing, decreed that every newborn Israelite son be drowned in the Nile. But Moses' mother evaded the order by putting her baby in a rush basket and hiding him among the reeds growing alongside the riverbank, where the pharaoh's daughter found the infant. Touched by the pitiful cries she heard as she peered into the basket, she ordered the child saved and reared at the palace. When Moses reached manhood, the story continues, he observed the desperate condition of the enslaved Israelites and was inspired by the god of his forefathers to lead them out of Egypt.

The story of Moses, like the stories of the patriarchs told in the Book of Genesis, bears evidences of historical truth. For one thing, the very name Moses associates him with Egypt; the word is Egyptian and means "born of" or "the son of." In various spellings it appears as an element in the names of several Egyptian pharaohs—among them Thutmose, whose name meant "the son of the god Thoth"; Ptahmose, meaning "the son of the god Ptah"; and even Ramses, an elided form of the name meaning "the son of the god Re." Other Israelites mentioned in the Bible bear Egyptian names: Phineas and Hophni, Moses' grandnephews, who appear in the Book of Samuel, are among them; so are Merari, possibly Aaron, and other members of the tribe of Levi.

The story has another major anchor in verifiable fact: the archeological record indicates that throughout much of the Second Millennium B.C. Egypt enjoyed unprecedented traffic with foreigners; some of these contacts were with Semitic tribes whose way of life, as described by the Egyptians, matches that of the Israelites as set forth in the Bible.

For most of its prior history Egypt had been—with some exceptions—a relatively closed community, less subject than Mesopotamia to invasion and immigration, and therefore less influenced by cultural change. Unaffected by Egypt's insularity, however, the desert nomads roamed among the oases between Canaan and Egypt, periodically entering Egypt as far as the delta. The Egyptians considered the eastern edge of this alluvial plain at the mouth of the Nile "the beginning of foreign lands and the end of Egypt."

The marshy land of the delta proper was a good place for grazing cattle, and on its outskirts grain almost always grew in abundance. An Egyptian scribe of the late 13th Century B.C., reflecting an attitude that prevailed among Egyptian officials throughout the period, wrote of "letting the Bedouin tribes of Edom pass the fortress of Merneptah"—meaning that the desert nomads were allowed to enter the eastern region of Egypt—"to keep them alive and to keep their cattle alive." Another scribe noted that the nomads did this "after the manner of their fathers' fathers," reflecting a long-standing pattern.

Occasionally, when times were hard elsewhere —that is to say, when rainfall was inadequate farther north—the nomads might linger in and around the delta, just as the Bible says Jacob's sons did. But even then they tended to keep to themselves, not mixing with the native population, as their distant kin in Mesopotamia and Canaan repeatedly did; they generally left the delta when the crisis passed.

The nomads' standoffishness while on Egyptian territory may have been a necessary posture; while the Egyptians of this period permitted foreigners to encroach on their boundaries, they did not welcome them. Neither, in early times, were the Egyptians inclined to venture outside their own borders, which enclosed an elongated kingdom that stretched from the first cataract of the Nile, at Aswan, 750 miles north to the river's mouth. But circumstances of the Second Millennium B.C. altered Egypt's isolationism. The stepped-up migratory movement that was taking place elsewhere in the Near East led more and more peoples in Egypt's direction; and Egypt in turn was lured into international trade and empire building.

The first important newcomers to penetrate Egypt's boundaries were the Hyksos, a warlike people of mixed Semitic and Indo-European origin, who arrived in the middle of the 17th Century B.C. They settled themselves in lower Egypt and took over much of the region by default: the pharaoh's authority, centered in the ancient city of Thebes, was weak in the region of the delta. In time the Hyksos set up their own capital at Avaris. Thus, 2,500 years after the founding of Egypt's First Dynasty, a rich part of the kingdom fell under non-native rule.

A Pharaoh's Own Monotheism

Until the mid-13th Century B.C., when Moses led the Israelites out of Egypt, no other people of the ancient world had worshipped a single, all-powerful god; in Egypt, as elsewhere, the people venerated many gods. However, a century before the Exodus, the pharaoh Akhenaton made a brief, doomed attempt to impose upon his subjects one deity as supreme ruler of the universe—a spirit called Aton, whose earthly son was the pharaoh and whom only he and his queen could worship directly.

Some scholars have seen Akhenaton's devotion as the first manifestation of monotheism. But Aton was a self-evident natural force and Akhenaton, his only priest, was himself considered divine; whereas the one god of the Israelites was an all-powerful being and Moses, a mortal, was deemed his chosen interpreter. In Akhenaton's zeal to establish Aton and force the people to worship only himself as Aton's manifestation on earth, the pharaoh built a new capital at a site now called Tell el-Amarna. There, oblivious to the futility of his mission, Akhenaton served Aton in growing isolation, neglecting his governmental duties and allowing the economy to slide toward ruin. At his death, his successor to the throne reverted to a pantheistic orthodoxy.

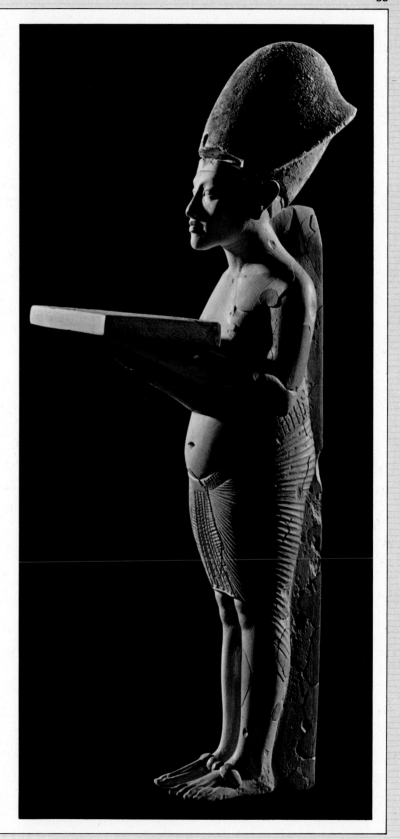

As incised in this scene on an altar panel at left, Pharaoh Akhenaton and his queen, the fabled beauty Nefertiti, play with three of their daughters while basking in the divine rays of the god Aton, represented by the sun disk. A statue of the king at right holds a tray bearing offerings to Aton. Both the statue and the altar panel were made of limestone in the mid-14th Century B.C., and are about 16 inches high.

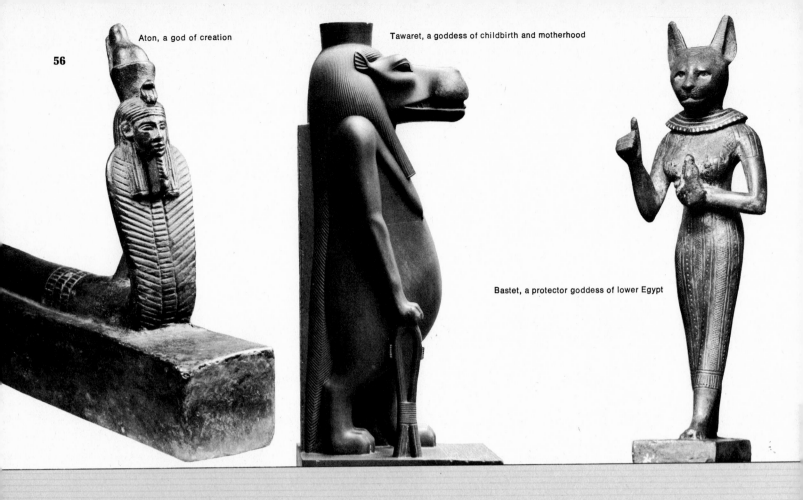

Aton, a god of creation

Tawaret, a goddess of childbirth and motherhood

Bastet, a protector goddess of lower Egypt

The phenomenon of foreign intrusion was an aberration that lasted relatively briefly—a century—but it permanently marked the Egyptian nation in a number of ways. Some time around 1560 B.C. a native dynasty reasserted itself, drove the Hyksos out and returned the capital to Thebes. But the newcomers had left the Egyptians the horse and chariot—and a new appetite for foreign expansion of their own.

When Thutmose III came to the throne in 1490 B.C., he pushed the limits of Egyptian control eastward. They eventually reached as far as the Euphrates Valley, making most of Canaan and part of Syria an Egyptian province. It is at this time that the name Canaan makes a first appearance in written records.

The Egyptians who carried out the pharaoh's expansion indulged themselves, in the time-honored way of soldiers everywhere, at the natives' expense. One scribe of Thutmose's reign wrote of the expedition into Canaan: "Behold, the army of his majesty was drunk every day as at a feast in Egypt." Another wrote that they took home "every pleasing thing of the country": incense, wine and cattle; chariots and armor; precious stones, gold and silver. And among the booty they carried away were human captives, whom they put to work as slaves in Egypt—a practice that continued under succeeding pharaohs for the next 300 years. Some of these Canaanite captives may have been the ancestors of the slaves whom Moses was to lead out much later.

In 1290 B.C. Ramses II came to the throne. During his extraordinarily long reign of 65 years, the shadowy history of the Israelites becomes a little more discernible. By comparing Biblical passages with Egyptian records of his reign, scholars have been able to approximate the period when the Israelites suffered forced labor in Egypt, and to guess at the time of their departure under Moses' leadership. The estimates place the Exodus toward the end of the 13th Century B.C.—either at the end of Ramses' rule, or possibly when the next pharaoh ascended the throne.

Indeed, that period appears to have been opportune for the escape of a subject people. Though the

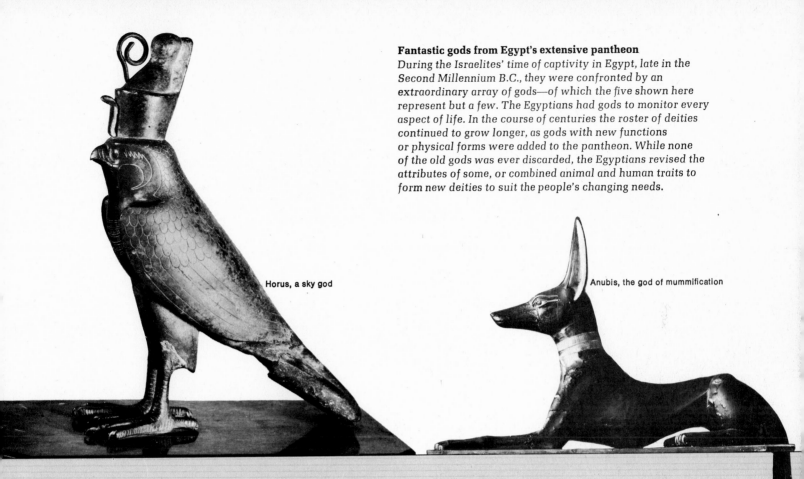

Horus, a sky god

Anubis, the god of mummification

Bible does not mention it, Egyptian records reveal that the latter part of the century was a time of growing troubles for the pharaohs. In the delta region immigrants from Libya, the arid land to the west of Egypt, were encroaching. On Egypt's Mediterranean shore the first contingent of a new wave of seaborne invaders was sailing in from the north and west. By 1200 B.C. the invading Sea Peoples had made a shambles of the Hittite Empire, and the people identified in the Bible as the Philistines were beginning to take over the coast of Canaan.

So, in the turbulent quarter century between 1225 and 1200 B.C., a great many foreigners who had earlier been enslaved by Egypt managed to flee their distracted captors. Among them may have been some who, moving to safety in Canaan, brought with them a memory of deliverance by a man named Moses.

It is doubtful that these Semitic settlers in Canaan were linear descendants of the patriarchs depicted in Genesis, or that they came in a single body. More likely they were later strains of nomadic Semites who

merged with other Semitic tribes already in Canaan; in time their separate tribal memories focused on a common antipathy for the Egyptians. That emotion could have been felt by those who had never been in Egypt itself; Egyptian rule in Canaan, though suffered only sporadically, and not altogether oppressive, had been for the most part a painful burden.

For those who had actually been in Egypt, oppression was real enough. Ramses, who undertook the most ambitious construction program Egypt had seen since the days of the pyramid builders a millennium and a half before, conscripted foreigners to do all kinds of work for the empire: to man the army, especially the remote garrisons along the northeast trade route into Canaan; to till the fields and vineyards; to pave roads, erect temples, build a new palace and construct two virtually new cities. Among his many projects, Ramses built the great temple at Abu Simbel, where four colossal statues of himself, 67 feet high, overlook the Nile.

Both the Bible and Egyptian records corroborate

During the Exodus from Egypt, Moses carries out the orders of his god, symbolized by the hands at the top of this 244 A.D. fresco. At left, he leads the oppressed Israelites across the Red Sea, just drained by divine intervention so that the remaining shallows teem with jumping brown fish. Lined up behind the vanguard of troops are the elders of the traditional 12 Israelite tribes. At right, a second image of Moses appears in the act of flooding the Red Sea again—now that the Israelites are safe in the desert—thereby engulfing the Egyptians who pursued them. The four-foot-high fresco, only

a portion of which is reproduced here, was found in the ruins of a synagogue at the Syrian city of Dura-Europos by a British patrol during World War I. The picture had unwittingly been preserved by the city's inhabitants in 256 A.D.; the temple was located close to the town walls. In a last effort at defense against an advancing enemy, the citizens tore the roof from the building and filled the rooms with sand to make a deep barrier. Because of the protective sand pack, when the British dug out the synagogue the fragile paintings emerged almost unscathed by the passage of some 17 centuries.

the theory that much of the work accomplished in the reign of Ramses was done by forced labor. An Egyptian panel of frescoes found at Thebes shows slaves making bricks. They moisten clay with water, add straw, knead the mixture and carry it in baskets to wooden molds, in which bricks are pressed into shape and then dried in the sun. The Bible underscores the oppression with details so telling that they become major insights: "Pharaoh ordered the people's overseers and their foremen not to supply the people with the straw used in making bricks, as they had done hitherto. 'Let them go and collect their own straw, but see that they produce the same tally as before.'" Egyptian wall paintings show the foremen enforcing these orders by beating their charges.

Written records of Ramses' reign also recount the conscripting of foreigners to "haul stones for the great fortress of the city of Ramses." The Book of Exodus identifies at least one group of the foreigners: the Israelites, it says, "were made to work in gangs with officers set over them, to break their spirit with heavy labor. This is how Pharaoh's store cities, Pithom and Ramses, were built."

The second of these cities—called Per-Ramses by the Egyptians, meaning "house of Ramses"—was the old city of Avaris, the erstwhile capital of the Hyksos, renamed. Ramses reinstated it as the capital, partly because his family came from the region; he also preferred its climate to that of his predecessors' capital at Thebes, where it was too hot. Egyptian records describe Per-Ramses as a capital "full of food and provisions"—no doubt what the Bible meant by calling it a "store city."

Besides being a political power case and reposi-tory of provisions for the pharaoh, Per-Ramses was also a religious capital. Like other major cities of the kingdom, it reflected the deep religiosity that ran through the lives of all Egyptians, from the pharaoh on down. In concept and practices it stood in sharp contrast to the Israelites' faith.

Each quarter of Per-Ramses featured a temple consecrated to a different god. And at the very center of the city, by deliberate plan, was the royal palace, the residence of the king, "a place of dazzling halls of turquoise and lapis lazuli," according to an Egyptian papyrus. For among the principal gods was always the pharaoh himself: the embodiment of all the powers of nature, the intermediary between earth and heaven, the symbol of universal order. One Egyptian who served Thutmose III in the 15th Century B.C. wrote of the pharaoh's divinity: "He is a god by whose dealings one lives, the father and mother of all men, alone by himself, without an equal."

However, there was still room for lesser gods. In Egypt, as in Mesopotamia, the pantheon had a cast of hundreds: gods of the earth, the sky, and each of the regions and towns of the empire; gods who ruled over the dead and gods who watched over the affairs of the living. For instance, the god Khnum was credited with bringing mankind into being on a potter's wheel; his wife, Heket, helped women in childbirth. The god Thoth presided over weights and measures; the goddess Ernutet was the patroness of food grains.

This pantheistic hierarchy prevailed throughout ancient Egypt's long history, except for one brief spell during the 14th Century B.C.; at that time the pharaoh Akhenaton made a short-lived attempt to introduce monotheism of a sort. His reform had no discernible antecedents or lasting impact. But be-

cause the concept appeared in a land where the Israelites spent so much time, its possible link to the development of monotheism has not been dismissed.

Akhenaton himself was, at best, a misfit. The pharaoh was a strange-looking man with a drooping jaw and outsized hips and thighs. What inspired his religious notions remains a mystery, but he undertook to promulgate the virtues of a single god, Aton; he decreed that Aton had created the world and "all men and cattle and wild beasts." Aton was the ultimate ruler of Egypt, of all foreign countries and of "the great green sea."

This deity represented a curious new departure in a land where most gods and their roles had a specific, concrete relationship to the people's lives; the god of the Nile, for example, was revered for the life-giving, yearly inundation of the river's banks that enabled the crops to flourish. By contrast, Aton was an abstract deity—never represented in the animal or human forms that Egyptians were accustomed to worship. Aton could only be seen as the sun disk that passed above Egypt each day, overseeing everything he had created. His dominion was total; no phase of life was too vast or too minute for his attention. "When the chick in the egg speaks within the shell," says a hymn written by Akhenaton, "thou givest him breath within it to maintain him."

So zealously did Akhenaton embrace his own invention that he tried to stamp out all the gods that his fellow Egyptians had cherished since time immemorial. Not content with denouncing them orally, the pharaoh sent workmen armed with hammers and chisels to all the ancient temples and tombs in Egypt to deface inscriptions honoring other gods, substituting Aton's name and taking special care to erase the hieroglyphs for the plural word "gods."

Akhenaton's iconoclasm did not outlast the king himself. When he died, about 1350 B.C., his religion died with him. Brief as Akhenaton's obsession was, some scholars speculate that his focus on one god —unique at the time—may have provided seed for Moses' ideas, which were to rouse the Israelites scarcely a century later.

But the weight of expert opinion falls heavily against this theory. For one thing, Aton, as the sun, was just one cosmic force; Yahweh ruled the entire cosmos. Secondly, Aton was visible every day; Yahweh sometimes temporarily took human form for the purpose of manifesting himself to a particular man at a special time, but from the beginning he was in conception a divine being without any form. And in Akhenaton's zeal to impose his cult on his subjects, he overlooked the element indispensable to popular acceptance: he deprived the people of the right to worship the god directly. Only he and his family, performing as the people's intermediaries, were allowed to revere Aton personally. The people were expected to abide by the ancient belief in the pharaoh's own divinity, which left unresolved the question of whether Akhenaton actually countenanced two gods—including himself—instead of only one. Finally, Akhenaton's cult did not address itself to ethical and moral principles as Moses' god did.

Indeed, there is much evidence that, far from being Egyptian in origin, the idea of the personal god is Semitic. In Exodus, the Israelites' god comes into sharp relief and takes on some new characteristics.

First, he has acquired the name Yahweh. In ancient Hebrew—whose alphabet had few, if any, vow-

Idols That Vied with the One God

Wherever the Israelites' wanderings took them in the ancient Near East they encountered the worship of bulls. The beast, revered for its virility and fearsome strength, was often seen either as a god in its own right or as a worthy gift for deities. In Mesopotamia the bull symbolized fertility, storms and even heaven itself. In Egypt it was variously revered as a fertility god, as a guise of the sun god and, ultimately, in the form of Apis-Osiris, as lord of immortality and eternity. Canaanites expressed their piety by burying a bovine effigy in the foundation of a temple. Thus, inevitably, when the Israelites' faith flagged—as Exodus reports it did—and they felt the need of an idol to bow to, their priest, Aaron, fashioned a bull of gold.

Between lyre-shaped horns, Apis-Osiris, the Egyptian bull god of Memphis, carries a sun disk and heraldic viper, which were worn together as symbols of the power of solar deities. Less than six inches high, this bronze statuette was made during the Sixth Century B.C.

Sculpted of glowing alabaster, this lifelike bull's head, eight inches high, was left unadorned except for the inlays of dark stone that are its eyes. The work of a Sumerian artist in Mesopotamia, it was carved early in the Third Millennium B.C. and was probably made as a votive offering for one of Sumer's many gods.

Evocative of the heretical idol made by Aaron, the Israelite priest, a young bronze bull, 15 inches long, wears a battered coat of gold. Fashioned in the Second Millennium B.C., it comes from the city of Byblos where Canaanite worshippers buried it along with the cornerstone of a sanctuary.

els—the word is written YHWH, and the same four consonants occur in different forms of the Hebrew verb "to be." This fact has led some scholars to link the name to various concepts of being.

By the Biblical account Moses, standing with his hands in front of his face to shield it from the radiance of the vision before him, asks his god: "If I go to the Israelites and tell them that the God of their forefathers has sent me to them, and they ask me his name, what shall I say?" The answer in the original Hebrew text is cryptic; it reads *Eheyeh-asher-Eheyeh*. Since the dawn of Biblical study and translation, that answer has been rendered with variations of phrasing; but it has always conveyed the same general sense: "I AM; that is who I am. Tell them that I AM has sent you to them."

Scholars have filled pages on the meaning of that enigmatic phrase, and on the name Yahweh that derives from it; but they can come to no agreement. One theory is that YHWH meant "I am" in the sense of everlasting existence. The important point, however, is that by the time YHWH was committed to writing—which did not happen for at least 200 years after the desert journey, during which the name first came into use—the Israelites themselves had probably already lost track of the original meaning; they held the name Yahweh sacred simply because it designated their god.

They also incorporated it extensively in naming their children, following a common practice of the times. Like the Egyptian pharaohs Thutmose, Ptahmose and Ramses, Near Easterners generally made extensive use of their gods' names in their own. For example, the Assyrian king Ashurbanipal's name incorporates that of the god Ashur. The Israelites applied the name of Yahweh to their priests and prophets as well as to their offspring—either as a way of invoking the god's favor for the individual or of offering a prayer of thanks. Familiar examples, in which the last element of the name—*iah*—is a form of Yahweh, include Hezekiah (meaning "Yahweh is my strength"), Jeremiah ("May Yahweh lift up") and Nehemiah ("Yahweh has comforted").

Yahweh identifies himself by that name near the beginning of the Book of Exodus. He signals Moses that it is time to assert his divine power over the ruler of Egypt and force the pharaoh to release the Israelites from bondage. The pharaoh resists this claim of divine authority—made by Moses and supported by his brother Aaron—and refuses to let the Israelites go. Thereupon Yahweh sends a succession of misfortunes and plagues to exact the pharaoh's consent. These legendary evils, 10 in all—including infestations of frogs, maggots and flies, boils, hail and locusts—do not force the pharaoh's capitulation. Only when Yahweh causes the death of all Egyptian first-born children does the pharaoh relent, though he changes his mind yet again. After the Israelites have begun their journey under the leadership of Moses, the pharaoh sends soldiers to overtake them.

The pharaoh risks increasingly dire punishment by standing up to the will of Yahweh, but his stubbornness is to no avail. The escape of the Israelites and the subsequent destruction of their pursuers confirms for the Israelites the overwhelming power of their god against what from time immemorial had been regarded as an irresistible force: the religious authority of the pharaoh himself. In the course of achieving this victory, Yahweh has extended his protection to the whole nation of the Israelites and thereby establishes himself as superior to the pharaoh and to all the gods worshipped by the Egyptians. Furthermore, the Israelites find in the victory confirmation of the covenant with their god made by their forebears.

For all the religious significance of this aspect of the Exodus narrative, the story rests on the most speculative foundation—at least when it deals with the flight itself. The Israelites' route from Egypt is far from easily located (page 69). Escaped slaves were a frequent problem for the Egyptians, who usually pursued the fugitives in the desert. "Write me all that has happened," one anxious Egyptian official commanded a subordinate making such a chase in the 13th Century B.C. "Who found their tracks?"

Try as they will, archeologists cannot find the tracks of the Israelites. In making their plans, the escapees would presumably have had intelligence on the best—or, at any rate, the least perilous—ways to travel. The shortest route from Egypt to Canaan would have been the trail running up the Canaanite coast that was used by traders—a fact that is noted in the Biblical account, which goes on to say: "God did not guide them by the road toward the Philistines." That statement is a 10th Century B.C. anachronism edited into the story; in the 13th Century B.C. the Philistines had not yet consolidated their hold on the Canaanite coast. But there would have been good reason to avoid the coast, since fortified cities stood along the way, manned by soldiers able to prevent the passage of fugitives.

So instead of that hazardous route, says the Bible, "God made them go round by way of the wilderness toward the Red Sea." Modern scholars are certain that this is not a reference to the Red Sea designated on today's maps. For one thing, they have traced this reading of the name to an error made by Third Century B.C. Greek translators; the text should say "Reed Sea," or "Sea of Reeds," which is the way it is translated in the 16th Century A.D. version by Martin Luther, who worked from the Hebrew text. Indeed, Luther's translation is borne out by geography; the Red Sea lies so far south of the Nile Delta, from which the Israelites set out on foot and on donkeyback, that they never would have reached it. The Egyptians, using speedy horses and chariots, would have overtaken them long before Moses' famous exploit—the parting of the waters so that the Israelites could safely walk across. An approximation of this incident is much more likely to have taken place in the area of the modern Suez Canal, at the time a region of shallow lakes that could have been forded.

When the Israelites reach the place the Bible calls Mount Sinai—in some passages named Mount Horeb —Moses first transmits to his followers the Ten Commandments. That much is clear from Exodus, but the actual site of this significant point in the narrative is almost impossible to pin down. The mountain could correspond to any of several sites in the southern end of the Sinai Peninsula. One reason for placing it there is that the area has many copper mines, and the clan into which Moses married practiced metalsmithing—an obvious craft in a mining region.

Another plausible site for the Biblical Mount Sinai would be at the tip of the Gulf of Aqaba on the northern fringe of the Arabian Desert. Geological evidence can be invoked to support this theory, which helps explain the dramatic scene in which the Bible relates the people's first hearing of the Ten Commandments: "Mount Sinai was all smoking, because the Lord had

A Traditional View of Moses' March

Leading 600,000 Israelites in massed formations, Moses (lower right) walks beside the sacred Ark of the Covenant. This extremely romanticized engraving, by a 17th Century A.D. German artist, was inspired by the Bible's description of the march through the wilderness—today's Sinai desert.

Directly behind Moses are the Levites, the tribe assigned to protect the ark. The three close-ranked units behind them are the tribes of Issachar, Judah and Zebulun. Women, children and cattle follow among the covered

wagons—carrying parts of the disassembled tabernacle—all guarded on both flanks. Trailing behind are four groups of Levite soldiers.

Opposite the point where the cliff juts into the plain are the tribes of Reuben, Simeon and Gad, followed by their own protected complements of relatives and baggage. Of the next orderly phalanx of three, two units are led by Ephraim and Manasseh —contingents of the same tribe of Joseph—and the third is commanded by Benjamin. They, too, precede their guarded families and baggage train.

The last three of the 12 tribes belong to Asher, Dan and Naphtali. Bringing up the rear are the stragglers —the sick and crippled—plus non-Israelite refugees from Egypt who had attached themselves to the march.

come down upon it in fire; the smoke went up like the smoke of a kiln. Whenever Moses spoke, God answered him in a peal of thunder."

To many scholars the scene raises the possibility that Moses' message to his followers was accompanied by a volcanic eruption. To people who had never seen or heard of a volcano, such an occurrence would certainly be mysterious, awesome and explicable by no less a phenomenon than the visitation of an all-powerful deity. The region today called Sinai has little evidence of volcanic action, but the Arabian Desert is spotted with extinct volcanoes.

Wherever Mount Sinai may in fact have been, in legend the place was of climactic importance to the Israelites by virtue of the commitment made there by all the people to abide by the Ten Commandments. After elaborating on the laws, the Bible relates: "The whole people answered with one voice and said, 'We will do all that the Lord has told us.' " With that pledge, they followed in the footsteps of their ancestors, renewing the covenant with their god, promising worship in exchange for divine protection.

As is often the case at a major turning point in human history, the participants in this event were both honoring inherited traditions and adding to them an epochal new construction. In form, their pledge at Mount Sinai reaffirmed the covenant made by their forefathers. The new construction was the Ten Commandments: the unconditional demand for ethical behavior—placed not on the shoulders of a king, or even of a patriarch on behalf of his constituency, but on every individual in the Israelite family.

To be sure, the concept that there was a price to be paid for misconduct was not an innovation. The Su-

merians had perceived the suffering of misfortune as divine punishment for bad behavior and had sought to atone for it by means of priestly ritual. The Babylonians had instituted laws providing punishment for wrongs, including one that instructed "if a man has caught a man with his wife, and a charge is brought and proved against the accused, both the wife and her lover shall be put to death." Based on such principles, already existing legal codes in the Near East had provided increasingly complex and explicit lists of crimes and the penalties for them. But to say, as in the Ninth Commandment, "You shall not covet your neighbor's wife" was unprecedented. This approach seeks out the private motives of wrongdoing, and for the first time in history rooted the law in the concept of moral responsibility. It made misconduct a matter for man to settle between himself and his god. That principle was to be fundamental to the future development of monotheism.

The god of the Commandments was invisible, without shape and impossible to represent, since he himself forbade it; but the fugitives who left Egypt and journeyed through the wilderness in search of the Promised Land came to believe, as they labored along, that an all-powerful divine spirit was traveling with them. To house this spirit they built a small portable shrine, which they called the Ark of the Covenant, and put it in the custody of the families claiming descent from Jacob's son Levi. To those accompanying it, the ark was a tangible guarantee that the Lord would keep his part of the divine covenant and deliver them safely through the wilderness to the Promised Land—which Moses never saw with his own eyes. His task, completed before he died, was to bring the Israelites to the threshold of fulfillment.

Charting the Trek to the Promised Land

Contemporary scholars and archeologists have tried to reconstruct the actual route taken by the Israelites as they escaped from bondage in Egypt and undertook the long trek through the desert wilderness. The possibilities are many and the clues are relatively few. However, close study and shrewd deductions, often made in the context of tradition, have served to narrow the main options to the four lines of march shown in color on the map at right. In each case the terrain the Israelites traversed some 3,000 years ago appears today much as it must have looked then: barren, rock-strewn expanses; dunes and grim mountains—relieved only by an occasional oasis.

Photographs of scenes that might well have surrounded Moses and his followers during the Exodus to the Promised Land in Canaan appear on the following pages. The precise spot where each picture was taken is located on the small map accompanying its caption.

Four possible Exodus routes, color-keyed on the map, begin at Ramses. From there confusion arises because there are at least three locations for the "Sea of Reeds"—where the pharaoh's pursuing army stalled. Also, references to Mount Sinai, where Moses proclaimed the Ten Commandments, fit no fewer than six peaks on the Sinai Peninsula alone.

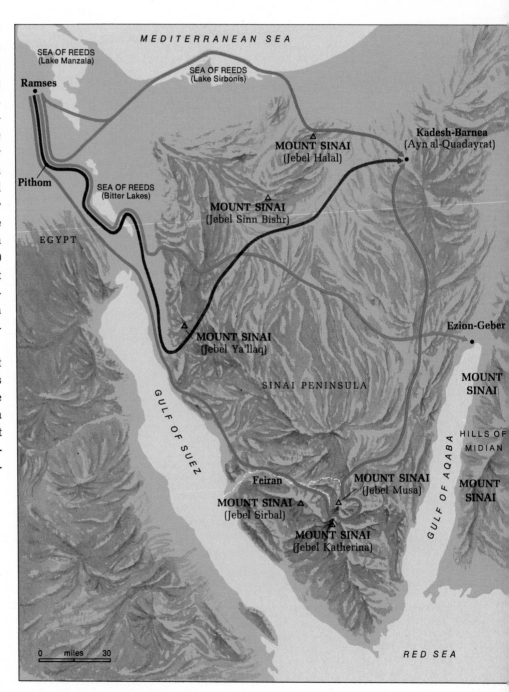

MEDITERRANEAN SEA

SEA OF REEDS (Lake Manzala)

SEA OF REEDS (Lake Sirbonis)

Ramses

MOUNT SINAI (Jebel Halal)

Kadesh-Barnea (Ayn al-Quadayrat)

Pithom

SEA OF REEDS (Bitter Lakes)

MOUNT SINAI (Jebel Sinn Bishr)

EGYPT

MOUNT SINAI (Jebel Ya'llaq)

Ezion-Geber

SINAI PENINSULA

MOUNT SINAI

GULF OF SUEZ

HILLS OF MIDIAN

GULF OF AQABA

MOUNT SINAI

Feiran

MOUNT SINAI (Jebel Musa)

MOUNT SINAI (Jebel Sirbal)

MOUNT SINAI (Jebel Katherina)

RED SEA

0 miles 30

"Red Sea" or "Sea of Reeds"?

An arm of the Red Sea, the Gulf of Suez (above) was long mistaken—because of a Biblical mistranslation—for the "Sea of Reeds" that aided the Israelites' escape from Egypt. But the tidal gulf is too deep and wide for fording.

Near the Mediterranean, a salt lagoon
—capable, in wetter times, of supporting
long-stemmed grasses—is one likely
"Sea of Reeds." Crossing on a sand bar
(background), the Israelites could
have avoided Egyptian outposts.

At the time of the Exodus, a rush-
choked marsh probably filled the area
now called Bitter Lakes. A breakout
here would have afforded the Israelites
a choice of relatively short routes east
over the plateau of central Sinai.

Long Years in a Parched and Stony Wasteland

Beneath a wind-battered mountain scarp, a dry stream bed—or wadi—carves a canyon across south Sinai. Israelites passing this way would have risked encounter with Egyptian patrols at nearby turquoise mines.

Hardpan gravel alternates with drifted dunes in north-central Sinai. The Israelites would have found minimum forage here for their animals, and would have suffered from thirst between the scarce, widely scattered wells.

In southwest Sinai the ground is level, but strewn with boulders that make passage difficult. In the background to the south is a range of mountains, one of whose peaks may have been the Mount Sinai of the Bible account.

Respites at Desert Springs and Streams

Acacia trees—the wood of which the Ark of the Covenant was made during the flight through the wilderness—flourish near Feiran, Sinai's largest oasis. The oasis is watered by springs and runoff from adjacent mountains.

A rivulet purls beside a grove of palms at the oasis called Kadesh-Barnea, whose name connotes a holy place. The oasis is a likely terminus of the Israelites' wilderness journey to the threshold of the Promised Land.

A spring dawn warms the gaunt summit of Jebel Musa, a 7,495-foot-high block of granite long associated with the Biblical Mount Sinai. The Old Testament was far more concerned with the sacred significance of Mount Sinai than with its location. Jebel Musa means "Mount Moses" in Arabic, and is sacred today to Muslims and Christians.

During a period of roughly 200 years—from before 1200 B.C. until some time after 1050 B.C.—the Israelites in Canaan passed through the oft-repeated human process of settling down from nomadism into an agricultural and urban life. The conversion was not easy. A loose agglomeration of tribes, the Israelites had grown too unwieldy to be kept under the direct control of patriarchal family heads; and as their community grew larger and more complex, they faced new social, political and religious problems.

The solutions required leadership of a new and different order. The Israelites' period of adjustment to life in Canaan was, essentially, the Biblical age of the judges—a new breed who were neither patriarchs nor kings but transitional leaders occupying a position between those roles. They were not judges in the exclusive, legal sense of the word. They were charismatic counselors who were endowed with the talents of sage, priest and military commander. In times of trouble the judges set the Israelites on the right path, either by mobilizing a fighting force, or by wise counsel, or both. Their roles were not hereditary and carried no legal sanction; it was assumed that their wisdom came as a blessing from their god.

Nevertheless, with the advent of the judges the Israelites began to move inexorably in an unanticipated direction: toward monarchy. For centuries they had

Two Canaanite figurines, both less than a foot high and made about the time of the Israelite conquest of Canaan, help substantiate the factual accuracy of Biblical accounts. The garb of the 1200 B.C. ivory noblewoman supports a statement in Judges that Canaanite ladies wore lavish embroidered robes draped from the neck; the gilded 1200 B.C. male figure is a Canaanite deity—probably Baal, whom the Bible often mentions as a false god to be shunned by the Israelites.

looked with suspicion on the notion of a single all-powerful ruler—a sentiment that was a natural outgrowth of their independent and self-reliant existence as nomads. To the wandering and fragmented early Israelites, power was a homely concept, residing in the patriarch as head of the family unit, whether large or small. Now, however, in the increasingly settled communities of Canaan, the old system did not work. Whenever trouble loomed, a menaced tribe sought help from a wise man, a judge. Sometimes the influence of the judge extended over only a single tribe, sometimes over several.

The most famous judges were those who by force of arms saved the Israelites from their enemies. These men of action emerge in the Bible as the heroes of some of the world's best-known adventure tales. Among the towering figures are Joshua, at whose command the walls of Jericho came tumbling down; and Samson, who had the strength to tear lions limb from limb until Delilah treacherously clipped his hair and robbed him of his power. Such characters—all from the books of Joshua, Judges and Samuel—have been celebrated in songs and poems, paintings and sculptures, for 3,000 years.

If these heroes are not real, in the sense that some books of the Bible are written compilations of ancient legends, nonetheless the resulting rich tapestry of fables is supported by a strong factual fabric. Their outsized exploits are eulogized in the context of larger themes: reward and punishment, right versus might, wit against brawn, and brawn against wealth. The themes themselves obviously were addressed to real problems that had to be solved by real persons. In that sense, Joshua and Samson and all the other valiant men glorified in the Biblical episodes devoted

80

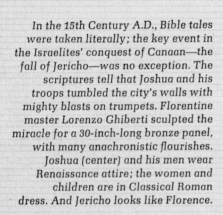

In the 15th Century A.D., Bible tales
were taken literally; the key event in
the Israelites' conquest of Canaan—the
fall of Jericho—was no exception. The
scriptures tell that Joshua and his
troops tumbled the city's walls with
mighty blasts on trumpets. Florentine
master Lorenzo Ghiberti sculpted the
miracle for a 30-inch-long bronze panel,
with many anachronistic flourishes.
Joshua (center) and his men wear
Renaissance attire; the women and
children are in Classical Roman
dress. And Jericho looks like Florence.

to the age of the judges represent heroes—perhaps
in composite—who actually lived. And as they accomplished their feats, they helped bring about
radical changes in the life style and power structure
of the Israelite tribes.

The Bible has it that, after the Exodus and many years
of desert wandering, "all Israel passed over" the Jordan River under the leadership of Moses' appointed
heir, Joshua, "to go in to occupy the country which
the Lord your God is giving you to possess." Having
crossed the Jordan, the narrative continues, the people stormed and captured the Canaanite city-states
—first Jericho and subsequently 31 others. This
accomplished, Joshua gathered the Israelites at Shi-
loh, where they worshiped at the ark. The tribes
then drew lots for territories to occupy and dispersed
to their allotted sites throughout the land.

The fanciful account of the fall of Jericho's walls,
while never documented by scholars, nonetheless
symbolizes accurately enough the crumbling of Canaanite power at approximately the time the Israelites settled there—though by no means was all the
takeover accompanied by warfare. Neither is it likely that the Israelites moved in with one quick,
decisive blow, with a single leader like Joshua heading a united people.

To be sure, archeologists have found numerous
signs that in the late 13th and early 12th centuries
B.C. fiery destruction overtook a number of Canaanite cities—among them Lachish, Beth Shemesh,
Hazor and Laish. Eventually new settlements, controlled by Israelites, rose on the ruins of the older
Canaanite ones. These Israelite cities differed in
character from their Canaanite predecessors; for one
thing the Israelite artifacts were much less sophis-

ticated: sickles of flint instead of metal, for instance, and crude pottery. That, indeed, would be the case in the settlements of a people lately come from nomadism into a new land and a new way of life.

But archeologists have also found the foundations of villages on sites that had never been occupied before 1200 B.C. Such discoveries suggest that the Israelites probably did not come into Canaan in a single body, as the Bible states, attacking the cities in their path. More likely, the Israelites trickled in tribe by tribe, or even clan by clan, coalescing after they arrived, and probably causing little disturbance at first among the Canaanites and other resident peoples. They located in the unpopulated sections of the countryside around and beyond the cities. The new arrivals cleared the forests and settled down to farm, weave and make pottery. Not until later did they run afoul of the local powers, at a time when the

Canaanite city-states were on the wane and the Israelites themselves were so well established that they had vested interests to protect—and felt secure enough to venture conquests of their own.

The Israelites settled more or less in clusters among enclaves of non-Israelites, and in four different regions: west of the Jordan River—north to south —were Galilee, Ephraim and Judah; east of the river lay Transjordan. These geographic separations account for the Biblical statement that not all the tribes participated in confrontations with a common enemy and also explain why, from time to time, the tribes themselves were at odds with one another. Despite these separations, however, throughout the 12th and 11th centuries B.C. a culture was evolving in Canaan that was to emerge as uniquely Israelite.

Again, evidence from archeological sources coincides with random, corroborating clues in the Bible it-

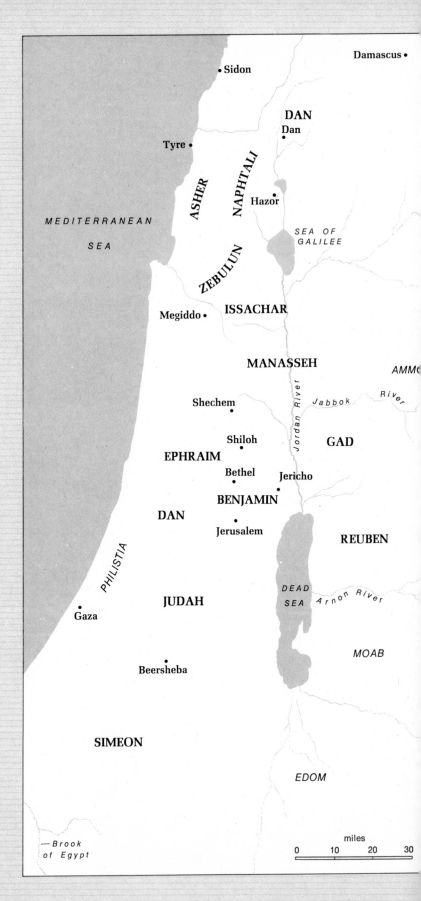

self. One passage, for instance, refers to "the clans of the guild of linen workers" among the tribe of Judah; and in the southern section of Canaan—the region the Bible allots to the tribe of Judah—excavations have uncovered looms and dye vats at Tell Beit Mirsim, which may well be the ancient site of Debir. Archeologists believe that the Judahites, a strong and numerous tribe, settled without much difficulty and that their solid entrenchment paved the way for the leading role they were later to play among the Israelite tribes.

In the northern region of Canaan, a number of tribes may have settled on land that was set aside for them in exchange for voluntary servitude to the incumbent ruler of the region. Some scholars suggest that one of those groups was the tribe of Issachar, who lived near the city of Megiddo. The very name Issachar may derive from an ancient Semitic word meaning "hired servant." An early Biblical passage describes the tribe of Issachar as "a gelded ass" —hardly a compliment, even in Biblical language, but not quite the insult such a description would be in modern speech. The term has reference to laborers at thankless tasks—donkeys being the beasts of burden of the time. Issachar, the Biblical account goes on to say, "saw that a settled home was good and that the land was pleasant, so he bent his back to the burden and submitted to perpetual forced labor."

There is a link in the archives of Egypt between the people of the Megiddo region in the north and the Biblical description of them as serfs. In the 14th Century B.C. the Prince of Megiddo communicated with his overlord, the pharaoh Akhenaton, giving an account of the construction that was underway. "Behold," he wrote, "I bring men for forced labor." For two centuries Megiddo had been a vassal of the Egyptian Empire. The archival fact that the area had been ruled by the pharaohs helps explain how Semites who lived outside Egypt and never actually suffered slavery there might have shared a traditional memory of Egyptian tyranny.

In any event, historians, archeologists and scholars see two major themes in the Biblical narratives that chronicle the time of the judges. The first of these is the welding together of a scattered collection of Israelite tribes in the face of several adversaries: the Canaanites, who were in the Promised Land before them; the Edomites, Moabites and Ammonites in kingdoms adjacent to Canaan, established only a short time before the Israelites; nomads who were following the Israelites into Canaan and were envious of their progress; and the Philistines, a branch of the Sea Peoples who settled the Canaanite coast and from there pressed eastward into the interior.

The other theme deals with the way the Israelites' view of their god and the worship they gave him underwent subtle adjustments as they shifted from a pastoral to an agricultural way of life. In matters of ritual the change led them to adopt some Canaanite practices—for instance, seasonal festivals celebrating the grape and barley harvests (pages 96-99). That development was logical; in their new agricultural pursuits they were for the first time bound up with the cycles of planting and harvesting, and so their worship fell into rhythm with their work. Such rites did not necessarily conflict with their devotion to the laws of Yahweh—although Canaanite gods, represented by idols, did attract some Israelites despite the ban against idolatrous worship.

Of more enduring importance than this flirtation with the ancient deities was a maturing conception of their own god and an emerging view of history as a continuous process in which they were fated to be an influence. History, as the Israelites saw it, was cyclical, and as time went on they cast the judges in important roles governing the cycle. They did not question that they had been granted the Promised Land by Yahweh in return for their worship. But despite the covenant, they grew careless from time to time and neglected the Commandments. As they finally came to perceive events, it seemed that in retribution for such neglect their god punished them by sending misery in the form of harassment by their enemies. Then when the Israelites repented and prayed to the Lord for deliverance, he would answer their prayers. "The Lord set judges over them, who rescued them," the Bible states.

After the judges put them back on the right track —either by leading them into battle to smite the foe, or by counseling the bravest and strongest in how to do so—the people would mend their ways in thanksgiving, and peace and prosperity would ensue for a number of years. But being forgetful, after a time the people would lapse again. The Bible continues: "And the Lord was angry with Israel and said, 'This nation has broken the covenant which I laid upon their forefathers and has not obeyed me.'" And so the cycle repeated itself.

This view of the Lord as a recurring protector is evident in the Song of Deborah from the Book of Judges. It is one of the oldest tales ultimately incorporated in the Bible. The song, a hymn of praise to the Lord for victory over the Canaanites, apparently was composed not long after the episode it commemorated, which makes it an early example of nearly contem-

Canaanite Prototypes for Solomon's Temple

Israelites of the Exodus must have seen numerous Canaanite temples. The ruins of two are shown on the page opposite; they are at the site of the city of Hazor, north of the Sea of Galilee. These 13th Century B.C. shrines were divided into three compartments: an antechamber, an inner room and, at the far end, a holy place where images of a god and votive offerings were kept. The great Temple of Jerusalem, commissioned by King Solomon in the middle of the 10th Century B.C., followed this familiar basic design.

In the Canaanites' view, a god actually dwelt in each sanctuary. But since the Israelites' god had no physical form, it needed no such earthly home. King Solomon erected his temple as a house for the sacred Ark of the Covenant, and thus reaffirmed Jerusalem as the spiritual—and political—focus of Israelite life.

This enthroned male deity—perhaps a moon or sun god—was unearthed in the Canaanite temple shown at bottom, opposite. Carved of basalt, the figure is seven inches high. Since the Israelites' religion banned images of their deity, the innermost chamber of their sanctuary held a pair of olive-wood cherubim, whose spread wings were meant to embrace the ineffable god.

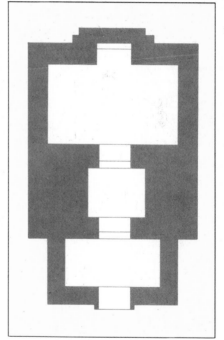

Digging at Hazor, archeologists uncovered at one temple a unique cache of basalt slabs and a sculpture resting on a raised platform. The 15-inch figure holding a bowl at the left is probably a Canaanite moon deity. The decorated slab at center features upraised arms surmounted by a crescent moon and disk, indicating that it may represent the moon god's consort.

A second shrine, whose floor plan is diagramed above, followed the Canaanites' standard three-chamber arrangement. This edifice was a modest prototype of King Solomon's monumental temple, erected some 300 years later. It was 75 feet long; Solomon's shrine measured over 140 feet. But the construction techniques were the same: each wall consisted of two rows of heavy stone with the space between filled with rubble.

porary history telling. And curiously, in a society so male dominated, the judge in this case was a woman.

Deborah was, by the Biblical account, valiant; she was also a seer, thought to be endowed with special wisdom. "It was her custom to sit beneath the palm-tree," the Bible relates, citing an ancient holy place near Bethel, "and the Israelites went up to her for justice"—meaning judicious advice as well as oracular guidance. So when the Israelites in the environs of the city of Hazor sought her counsel in defending themselves against the local ruler, Deborah sent for Barak, a wise warrior of the tribe of Naphtali, and ordered him to slay the Canaanites of Hazor.

It was a formidable assignment; Deborah's song goes on to say that the king's army commander, Sisera, had "900 chariots of iron," and "not a shield, not a lance was to be seen" among the Israelites. Again, the disparity in armament rests on the historical fact that the Israelites, unlike their contemporaries, had not yet caught up with Iron Age technology.

So Barak called for volunteers from his own tribe and the neighboring tribe of Zebulun—volunteers were the only resource of a people who had no standing army—and got 10,000 eager recruits. He assembled them on Mount Tabor, overlooking the plains below. Sisera, hearing that the Israelites were gathering, summoned his own men with their chariots and led them out to battle. Then, with some timely help from Yahweh, "the clouds streamed down in torrents," sluicing the plains with rain water, and the 900 chariots presumably were stalled by the mud. Barak, who had anticipated such divine intervention, swooped down the mountain "with ten thousand men at his back." The Canaanite Sisera abandoned his chariot and fled on foot, leaving his men and their horses to fend for themselves.

At this juncture in the story a second woman appears to help clinch the victory. Sisera sought refuge in the tent of a man named Heber, whom he held as an ally; but Heber was not there, and his wife, Jael, invited Sisera inside for a drink of milk, gave him a blanket, soothed him to sleep—and then, suddenly inspired to a shift in allegiance that was most welcome to the Israelites, drove a wooden tent peg into his skull. After that, says the Bible, the Israelites "pressed home their attacks upon that king of Canaan until they had made an end of him" and "the land was at peace for forty years."

Finishing off the king presumably involved the sacking of Hazor itself. And allowing for contradictions posed by other Biblical episodes, archeologists have found indications that Hazor was indeed destroyed around 1200 B.C. On that basis, its fall might well have come about after a victory such as the Song of Deborah commemorates.

Certainly there are sound historical reasons why the Israelites would have been able to defeat the Canaanites, not only in Hazor but elsewhere in the region. The Canaanite city-states had always been weak; they relied on the Egyptian Empire to the west and on the Hittite kingdom to the north for protection against other aggressors. But beginning in the late 13th Century B.C. both protectors became preoccupied with fighting off the onslaughts of the Sea Peoples and neglected the Canaanite cities. The Israelites moved into the power vacuum.

They remained secure for a time, but soon faced encroachment from the Midianites—a nomadic confederation that roamed the desert region bordering Canaan, just as the Israelites themselves had done in

This array of battle gear belonged to the Philistines, seafarers of mysterious origin who swept into the Near East around 1200 B.C. and—until their defeat by King David some 200 years later—violently disputed the Israelites' claim to Canaan. The items exhibited here, discovered at the sites of Philistine-manned garrisons along the coast, include an ornamental U-shaped spear butt, a dagger belt and a dagger. Except for the dagger blade, fashioned of iron, all the metal is bronze. (The spear itself was presumably made of wood and long since disintegrated.) The Philistines had a local monopoly on iron, which was cheaper and more abundant than the bronze of most Israelite weaponry, giving them a great initial advantage.

earlier times. The Midianites were not content to graze their flocks; they made periodic raids into Israelite territory west of the Jordan, ranging through the tilled fields, looting whatever they could and reappearing again the following year as soon as the next harvest was in. Appropriately—since the issue was the land's produce—the Biblical hero who rose to save the Israelites in this instance was a farmer's son named Gideon.

Gideon was threshing wheat inside his father's wine press, to keep it out of sight of the raiders, when a vision appeared to him. "You are a brave man, and the Lord is with you," Gideon heard the voice say. "Go and use this strength of yours to free Israel from the power of the Midianites."

Unlike Barak in the Song of Deborah, Gideon did not have to face an adversary advancing in a juggernaut of chariots; the Midianites were no more equipped with such sophisticated weapons than were Gideon's men. But the Midianites outnumbered his force by thousands—they "lay there in the valley like a swarm of locusts." And they had a brand new means of locomotion in the domesticated camel.

But like Barak before him, Gideon made up in strategy what he lacked in technology. He chose the best 300 men from the tribes of Manasseh, Asher, Zebulun and Naphtali—neighbors he could count on for bravery, obedience and stealth. He told each man to equip himself with a trumpet fashioned from a ram's horn, and a torch concealed inside a pottery jug.

Gideon divided his small force into three groups and stationed them on different sides of the Midianites' camp. Then at midnight, when the Midianites were busy with the changing of their guard, all 300 Israelites blew their trumpets on a signal from Gideon,

An eight-inch mold carved of stone enabled a Canaanite smith to mass-produce metal effigies of this female deity, shown here in a modern bronze reproduction. Her headdress features a conical hat and a pair of horns. Archeologists digging at the site of a 17th Century B.C. Canaanite holy place found two silver horns that fit precisely into the original form.

shattered their jugs noisily, simultaneously turning the field into a sudden blaze of light with their uncovered torches, and shouted "A sword for the Lord and for Gideon!" Presumably they also set fire to the camp and caused a stampede among the hapless camels. Gideon's enemies fled in confusion, mistaking friend for foe. "Throughout the camp the Lord set every Midianite man against his neighbor," while Gideon's force had nothing to do but watch.

When Gideon returned to his people after this triumph, they expressed their gratitude in a note new for the Israelites—one that was to echo softly, with scarcely noticeable effect, for some time thereafter. They invited him to become their king. "You have saved us from the Midianites," they exclaimed, "now you be our ruler, you and your son and your grandson." But Gideon replied: "I will not rule over you, nor shall my son; the Lord will rule over you."

After Gideon the desire for a king was not to disappear, though it would lie quiescent for a time. Meanwhile, through many subsequent tales like Gideon's, there threads a constant refrain: "In those days there was no king in Israel, and every man did what was right in his own eyes."

In a Near Eastern world that revolved around the central concept of rule by a king, the Israelites' attitude stands out in sharp relief. To this independent-minded people, still clinging to a deliberately loose tribal structure centered on a deity who directed all things and to whom each Israelite had direct access, submission to an earthly sovereign was both inconsistent with, and an intrusion on, that traditional and very personal relationship.

Yet all the circumstances of their lives were changing, as the very offer of a throne to Gideon indicates;

and with those changes were coming alterations in attitudes, customs and social organization. Inevitably, the Canaanites' ideas of government and religion had been a potent and pervasive influence on all the peoples who dwelt among them, including the Israelites.

The Israelites had largely abandoned their nomadic existence. They lived in houses of stone instead of tents. They had acquired property. The tribes were more closely bound together by mutual interests, proximity and more frequent contact. Their society was more stratified. In short, their new prosperity and close contact with the Canaanites had great impact on their culture. The story of an Ephraimite tribesman named Micah, as the Bible recounts it, bears careful study for the insights it provides into the evolution of Israelite civilization.

Many prosperous Israelites of the judges' time evidently built their own altars for worship at home. The Biblical narrative tells us that Micah had a shrine that was a part of his stone house. Perhaps the altar was in a separate room, or perhaps it stood in a courtyard. No one criticized Micah for having the shrine; family worship conducted by the father within the home, however humble, was a time-honored custom that went back at least as far as Abraham, and the custom survived long after Micah's time. But Micah went one step too far, violating the Second Commandment, which forbade the use of graven or molten images. Micah adorned his altar with two silver figures. He had them cast from 200 pieces of silver given him by his mother. The images would have been easy to commission, for the Canaanites were skilled at metalwork.

Micah's images are not described in the Bible, which significantly—in incorporating this folk epi-

sode—nowhere criticizes the man for an act that earlier generations would have labeled as a serious religious transgression. Some scholars speculate that, because the Israelites were influenced by the cultures newly surrounding them, one or both idols may have been in the form of a bull—a creature frequently deified in the Near East. But then Micah also hires a priest to tend his altar, saying, "I will pay you 10 pieces of silver a year and provide you with food and clothes." The sequence establishes that, even as early as the era of the judges, there had emerged among the Israelites a priesthood—professional men whose services were used both by individuals like Micah and at public places of worship.

Unfortunately for Micah, his priest left him for a more prestigious post with the tribe of Dan and took with him the silver idols. According to the narrative, the tribe of Dan "was looking for territory to occupy" —probably because it had been forced off its land by invaders. The significance to scholars of this passage in the narrative is the confirmation that this was an expansionist period for the Israelites. It also illustrates that their original areas of settlement were not always permanent, that tribes or clans changed locations from time to time as they encountered difficulties in the Promised Land.

The men of Dan prevailed upon the priest to steal Micah's silver idols, which they admired and wanted to use as altar furnishings. Their method of persuasion was adroit: "Come with us and be our priest and our father," they said to him. "Which is better, to be priest in the household of one man, or to be priest to a whole tribe and clan in Israel?" "This pleased the priest," the Bible notes, and this eminently practical spiritual leader accompanied the Danites

Charging Philistine warriors, their characteristic plumed helmets secured by chin straps, brandish lances and swords in this detail from a 12th Century B.C. Egyptian stone relief. The carving celebrates the victory of the pharaoh Ramses III over a coalition of seafarers, including the Philistines, that invaded Egypt, reaching the Nile Delta. Stopped by the pharaoh's armies, the Philistines headed for Canaan, where—in firm control—they resisted settlement by the Israelites.

to the Phoenician city of Laish, more than 100 miles away. The Danites stormed that city, took it over and renamed it Dan—a detail in the narrative that underscores how far the Israelites had progressed, in both physical might and psychological attitude, since the years in bondage. The Danites, the Bible continues, built a new place of worship for the silver idols, and prospered. Archeologists and Biblical scholars have been able to relate evidence from excavations at the site to the period covered by the Micah story —confirming that the city was indeed sacked.

By the middle of the 11th Century B.C. the scattered Israelite peoples faced a common enemy: the Philistines. The threat further stimulated the impetus toward consolidation—indeed made consolidation essential—and brought forward an archetypal Israelite judge. The judge was Samuel, and under him the course of the Israelites' history took a new turn.

Samuel was a priest who traveled from town to town, making an annual circuit of the altars at Bethel, Gilgal and Mizpah. But he was something more than a priest; a man of profound wisdom and foresight, he wielded great influence among the Israelites. He combined the roles of seer, prophet, judge and governor; and although he was not a military man, warriors came to him for blessings and for guidance.

The Philistines had come to Canaan early in the 12th Century B.C., after they were beaten back from the gates of Egypt by Ramses III. As seafarers, the Philistines at first contented themselves with occupying the Canaanite coast and gave the Israelites no trouble. They took up trading, installed military rule in the city of Gaza—a former Egyptian provincial capital—and in Ashkelon, Gath, Ashdod and Ekron,

joining the peoples of these cities into an alliance that soon dominated the southern coast of Canaan.

Like the Canaanites, the Philistines had an Iron Age technology that far outstripped the Israelites' crude skills and limited access to metals, and they meant to maintain their advantage. "No blacksmith was to be found in the whole of Israel," the Bible relates, "for the Philistines were determined to prevent the Hebrews from making swords and spears"—a note that signals the coming of conflict.

The trouble began with skirmishes here and there; but as the violence increased in frequency and severity, and broadened over a wider territory, the Israelite tribes increasingly began to feel the need for the coordinated action against the Philistines that only a strong central government could provide.

The Israelites had come a long way by now; some 200 years had passed since they left their nomadic desert life to take up agriculture in Canaan. They clung to the old tribal lore and to the pride of separateness that went with tribal loyalties. But the facts of desert life that had brought those convictions into being had been left behind. Now they had land to protect, food production to maintain, homes to keep safe and businesses to sustain. They also had developed a mutual identity that, if not yet quite national, now extended far beyond the tribe itself.

The earliest clashes—with Canaanites, with neighboring kingdoms and with nomads—had engaged only a few of the Israelite tribes at a time, but the defeat or emigration of one antagonist after another had secured a wider stretch of territory for the Israelites and reduced the gaps that separated the tribes.

To hold on to all their vested interests, the old patriarchal rule of the family no longer sufficed; neither was the rule of a judge over a handful of tribes enough—even when exercised by a judge of such renown as Samuel. The logical answer seemed to be a king, and Samuel was consulted on the matter.

The Bible describes the occasion: "So all the elders of Israel met, and came to Samuel and said to him, 'Appoint us a king who will govern us, like other nations.' But their request for a king to govern them displeased Samuel, and he prayed to the Lord. The Lord answered Samuel, 'Listen to the people and all that they are saying; they have not rejected you, it is I whom they have rejected, and I whom they will not have to be their king. Give them a solemn warning and tell them what sort of king will govern them.'

"Samuel told the people who were asking for a king all that the Lord had said to him. 'This will be the sort of king who will govern you. . . . He will take your sons and make them serve in his chariots and with his cavalry. . . . He will take a tenth of your grain and your vintage. . . . He will take a tenth of your flocks, and you yourselves will become his slaves.' . . . The people refused to listen to Samuel. 'No,' they said, 'we will have a king over us; then we shall be like other nations.' . . . So Samuel, when he had heard what the people said, told the Lord; and he answered, 'Take them at their word and appoint them a king.'"

Thus, out of their own keenly felt need, the Israelites came together for the first time in political unity under a monarch. Misgivings about kingship were to come back to haunt them, but for the next 100 years the monarchy was to give the Israelites earthly glory and a formidable place among the international powers of their day.

Sacred Rituals of Joy and Thanksgiving

From their earliest times, the Israelites set aside special days for religious observance. Three of those festivals—Passover, Shavuoth and Succoth—still highlight the modern Jewish calendar. The happiest Jewish holidays, they are also the oldest.

The newer ceremonies of contrition and atonement did not evolve until late in the Israelites' history. Yom Kippur—the Jews' most sacred and somber rite, a full 24 hours when they fast and pray for forgiveness of their sins—originated as a purification rite; it assumed new significance and forms after the Israelites were forced into exile by the Babylonians in the Sixth Century B.C. Rosh Hashanah, a cautious ushering in of the new year accompanied by deep self-scrutiny and a review of personal conduct in the year just past, began even later.

But the three exultant holidays, some rituals of which are shown on these pages, continue to be observed annually, preserving the exuberant spirits and timeless memory of the first years in the Promised Land.

On Passover eve three boys watch their father daub the doorway of their home with a marjoram sprig dipped in the blood of a lamb. The gesture recalls a time in Egypt when, according to Exodus, the Israelites' god slew the first-born male in every house—except for those clearly marked as Israelite.

Passover: Memory of Divine Deliverance

The focal events of a Passover in Canaan—the sacrifice of a lamb followed by a nocturnal feast—stemmed from a thanksgiving rite observed by the nomadic ancestors of the newly settled Israelite farmers. The shepherds had marked spring's arrival by offering to their god a male sheep or goat in gratitude for the fecundity of their flocks. The animal was roasted and entirely consumed the same night. After the settlement of Canaan, this ceremony—welcoming the season when nature seemed reborn—took on new meaning. Passover grew to commemorate the Israelites' own rebirth as a people, following their flight from Egypt. Thus, the menu—including unleavened bread and bitter herbs—symbolized aspects of the Israelites' years of oppression and their escape to freedom.

As his young son pays rapt attention, an Israelite father roasts the sacrificial lamb his family will eat that night at the Passover feast. The lamb is a yearling selected because it is healthy and unblemished; before it is cooked, its blood is let into a bowl for the lintel-marking ceremony (preceding page). The manner of its preparation follows rules set forth in Exodus: the bones must not be cracked nor the limbs severed, and it must not be boiled—for the scripture says, "Eat not it raw, nor sodden at all with water, but roast with fire."

Family members of all ages gather around the table to partake
of the carved roast lamb placed on a communal platter.
Rounds of unleavened bread are reminders of the people's
hasty departure from Egypt, when there was not time
to let bread rise before baking it. The men wear long robes and
bring shepherds' staffs to the table, reminiscent of the dress
and trappings of their nomadic forefathers. The Biblical text
specifically instructs that the Passover meal be eaten quickly
and that none of the lamb or the condiments be left over.

Shavuoth: Celebrating Spring's Harvest

The longest and perhaps the most joyful of all celebrations in the Israelites' year, Shavuoth was probably adapted from a Canaanite agricultural rite that the Israelites encountered when they first settled as farmers in the Promised Land. Beginning in the early springtime and continuing for seven weeks, Shavuoth was marked by two main ceremonies. In each farming community it started with a merry pilgrimage of all the families to a local sanctuary, where they made an offering to their god: the omer, the first sheaf of grain cut by each farmer at the beginning of the barley harvest. The close of Shavuoth culminated with another offering made by every family: two loaves of bread baked from the first yield of the wheat fields.

Filled with the joy of a good spring harvest—and responding to the balmy weather—villagers young and old set out with their offerings of omer. Some members of the casual parade carry the fresh-cut grain in their hands, others in baskets on their heads, and one leads a barley-filled ox-drawn cart. In the holiday spirit, some Israelites have adorned themselves —and even the oxen and the cart—with flowers picked from the profusion carpeting the countryside. The scene is set in the years shortly after the Israelites' settlement of Canaan, after 1200 B.C. Some 300 years later, the Shavuoth pilgrimage would take the worshippers to Jerusalem, where they would offer the omer in the temple newly erected by King Solomon.

Succoth: In Praise of Autumn's Gifts

The fall festival of Succoth—also called the Feast of the Ingathering—held a two-fold significance. Celebrated after the last of the autumn crops had been harvested, it was a time of gratitude for the fruitfulness of the land. At the same time, it served as one more reminder to the Israelites of their ancestors' journey out of Egypt when—in the wilderness of Sinai—they dwelt in tents or temporary lean-tos. Both of these meanings found expression during Succoth in the makeshift hut, called a *sukkah,* that each family built and decorated with the ripened fruits of the season. In these rustic booths, erected in orchards and vineyards, the Israelite families lived for the week that the festival lasted—feasting, enjoying the company of friends and singing praises to their god.

To build their sukkah (below), the men and boys of one family lay willow saplings against posts of cypress or acacia wood. When completed, the booth will have only three sides, walled with the palm fronds that the boys are setting in place. The roof will be loosely covered, permitting glimpses of the open sky as a reminder of the nomadic life and of man's dependence on the Almighty. Through the open side, the family will invite neighbors to join them in food and drink.

As the sukkah nears completion, the children begin to adorn the walls with the rich fruits of autumn—clusters of plump grapes, ripe pomegranates and pear-shaped, lemon-like citrons. More of these and other fruits that will be part of the Succoth feasting are arrayed on the table. The boy at right is holding a carefully selected citron, called the ethrog, and the lulav—a bouquet combining willow and myrtle branches with date-palm fronds. Symbolic of the earth's bountiful yield, the ethrog and lulav will be carried by male family members each time they convene to worship and sing songs of thanks.

Chapter Five: The First Kings

The Israelites entered a climactic era of their history toward the end of the 11th Century B.C. They turned to a soldier named Saul and inaugurated a monarchy as their new form of government. During his troubled reign, Saul stemmed incursions from foreigners —notably the Philistines—and thereby secured the land. His successors, David and Solomon, both of whom were more dazzling and ambitious, used the throne to transform the Israelites into a wealthy, increasingly integrated political force.

Most scholars believe there is a high degree of historical accuracy in the Biblical books that set forth the chronicles of these first three kings, although inevitably the stories are partly rationalizations by writers recording folk memories of events that took place long before their time. This conclusion is based on the regular pattern of correlation between archeological evidence and a close reading of the Biblical texts, which furnish considerable internal proof of their veracity.

Thus scholars are fairly certain that the Israelites had a king by 1000 B.C., though no one can be sure how long he reigned. By the Biblical account, Saul settled in a fortress capital at the town of Gibeah, and archeologists have excavated foundations of a fort in that town. Eventually Saul had under his command two full-time lieutenants, his son Jonathan and his cousin Abner; some experts interpret this or-

At Gibeon, just north of Jerusalem, a spiral staircase discovered in 1956 descends into a pool that was part of the ancient city's water system. Found in the reservoir were pottery fragments dating to 600 B.C. and inscribed with the name Gibeon; they confirmed that it was the exact site where the Old Testament says David triumphed over contestants for the Israelite throne and trounced his Philistine enemies.

ganizational development to mean that Saul had a standing army, the signal for a burgeoning kingship.

Archeological evidence of David's reign is scant, but scholars have found physical proof that certain events involving Saul and David took place where the Bible indicates they did. For instance, the remains of a large stone well have been found at Gibeon; the Bible refers to a "pool" at that spot in its description of a clash there between David's followers and those of Saul over the matter of succession.

The best substantiation that David actually existed derives from scrutiny of the Biblical passages recounting his life. He emerges from the pages as a rounded, totally human personality. Along with the recital of his accomplishments, David's misdeeds —including the story of the seduction of Bathsheba, wife of a subordinate—are objectively reported with no attempt at whitewash. Seen as a whole, the record presents a balanced picture of the king that carries the ring of authenticity.

The reign of the third Israelite monarch, Solomon, is linked by archeological investigation to ruined storehouses at Megiddo, Hazor and half a dozen other sites that bear his stamp as builder. And excavations in northern Jerusalem have provided confirming evidence that, as the Bible reports, Solomon extended the city's original limits during his time in power.

Along with the political and military expansion wrought by these earliest monarchs, their accessions unquestionably brought the Israelites the ornaments and complexities of higher civilization: monumental temples and palaces, foreign commerce with which to capitalize these and other construction enterprises, and a standing army to keep everyone safe. Particularly important was the promotion of writing skills.

The art was extended in scope from court annals to include prose and poetry of astonishing literary fullness and depth, much of it inspired by the institution of kingship; indeed, as creators of literature, the Israelites had few peers in the ancient world.

But the price of this wealth, cultural germination and security was submission to centralized authority. The prerogatives of the tribe and of its fatherly leader were displaced—as were those of the popular judges, who were personally known to everyone, whether the farmboy plowing his field or the shepherd watching his flocks—in favor of a remote and impersonal royal court. Equally significant, the new fiscal structure underpinning the material splendor of the monarchy produced a society that countenanced inequities between the mighty and the lowly, between the rich and the poor.

For the Israelites, these changes represented a radical departure from custom; though they had sought the monarchy, its coming generated severe pressures and conflicts. Over the next century, the struggle to resolve these conflicts, including the problem of royal succession, would sound a major theme in the development of the Israelites as a people.

When the tribes joined together proclaiming Saul their king, the Israelites were acting for the first time as a political body—though they did so in a religious framework. The Biblical text says that Saul was chosen king by the Lord through the agency of Samuel, the judge and priest whose sage counsel earned him widespread affection and loyalty among the tribes. Saul was the son of a well-to-do farmer of the Benjaminite tribe—a young man of modest demeanor and striking appearance: "as he took his stand among the people he was a head taller than anyone else." Samuel got his first look at the future king when Saul approached him for advice in finding some of his father's donkeys that had strayed.

Prompted by the voice of the Lord, who had earlier told Samuel that this was the man who "shall deliver my people from the Philistines," Samuel detained the youth. "Trouble yourself no more about the asses," he said, assuring Saul that they had been found. Then he told Saul of his sacred summons to greatness, placed the astonished and reluctant royal candidate in the seat of honor at his table and kept him under a host's supervision for the night. Next day Samuel anointed Saul, wetting his head with oil from a flask—a rite solemnizing divine participation in Saul's elevation to kingship. Soon the Israelites, assembled at Samuel's bidding, acclaimed their new leader, who was shyly hiding out of their sight and had to be fetched to acknowledge the joyous shouts of "Long live the king!"

However, the consciousness of his new role did not prevent Saul from the resumption of active farming—at least for a time. But his attitude and demeanor changed sharply when he faced his first military challenge. "Saul was just coming from the field driving in the oxen," the Bible relates, when he found his neighbors uttering lamentations; the Israelites to the north had been attacked. "The spirit of God suddenly seized him," the narrative continues. "In his anger he took a pair of oxen and cut them in pieces, and sent messengers with the pieces all through Israel to proclaim that the same would be done to the oxen of any man" who did not follow him into battle. Few disregarded the summons, and the army under Saul massacred the aggressors.

The reasons for the Almighty's choice of Saul to become monarch are not clearly explained in the Bible. But clearly the Philistines, with their professional army, iron technology and political solidarity, were a growing threat to the Israelites and there was immediate practical need for a military leader. Thereafter, social and political forces worked to make that leader a king. These realities appear in sharp silhouette between the lines of the Biblical text.

Thus seen, the experiences that befell Saul and his successors dramatize problems arising from the pull of entrenched tribal customs against the dynamic institutions and attitudes of royalty. For example, Saul's acclamation reveals primitive tribal democracy in action; this democracy was a powerful force, and future Israelite kings, unlike their neighbors in Egypt and Mesopotamia, would have to contend with it constantly.

Indeed, Israelite kings had a unique relationship with their subjects. Monarchs ruled over other Near Eastern peoples through a sort of common-law franchise that developed early in their political history. In those countries, kingship was older than writing, so there were no records to show it had ever had a beginning. Its end was unthinkable, and royal subjects looked upon the institution as divinely ordained, sacred and unchallengeable. Would-be kings might challenge incumbents for the throne, but kingship as such was taken for granted. For the Israelites, on the other hand, kingship was an institution they had deliberately sought. As they rationalized the situation, what they had asked the Lord to give, they could ask him to take away; what they had had a voice in acclaiming, they could just as well denounce.

In these circumstances, Saul had an unenviable

Among the deadliest weapons in the ancient world was the sling, a leather pouch hung on two long thongs. Crack slingsmen—like the Assyrians in the Seventh Century B.C. relief above or soldiers of the Israelite tribe of Benjamin —could accurately fire stone missiles as big as oranges (below) or hurl them from a valley floor into a fortified city.

task ahead of him. The diffidence that was appealing in Saul the lad was a liability in Saul the king, and the changes of mood he revealed before his first battle were to transform him into a tragic figure who would bring about his own undoing. The weight of his office, however, might have ruined a much steadier man than Saul. In a time of troubles he was elected as secular leader, a role complicated by the religious thrust of Israelite society. He had no precedents to guide or support him. The task required a strong man with a mind of his own, a gift for conciliation reinforced by a resolute will.

As his reign began, Saul's prospects looked promising enough. He had the majority of the people behind him, and for the time being he had the all-important support of Samuel. He commanded a willing levy of able troops, with whom he immediately won a stunning military victory. Moreover, as he devoted himself to his mission of defense, he was generally successful. He blocked intrusions by Moabites, Edomites and Ammonites—the peoples whose kingdoms lay to the east of the Israelites. He expelled marauders coming in from the desert. And he drove the Philistines from Israelite territories, holding them at bay in the coastal cities from which they had started, though his troops sustained some losses.

In victory, Saul's conduct as a military leader could be measured; he was not vindictive unless provoked. Canaanite cities still stood throughout the Israelites' territory, and he left them alone so long as they gave no trouble. He was not acquisitive; he added no territory the Israelites had not already claimed.

On the whole the Israelites were pleased to have Saul looking out for their interests; but one among them began to have second thoughts, and that was

Samuel. The first indication of trouble arose over a ritual sacrifice that Samuel was to perform for Israelite troops before a march against the Philistines. To get to the field of battle Samuel had to make a cross-country trek, and he arrived seven days late —just in time to find that Saul had gone ahead and performed the sacrifice on his own and had sent his men into the fray.

Samuel was stung; he regarded this initiative of Saul's as a usurpation of his priestly functions. Considered objectively, the act was probably justified. Performing a sacrifice without the aid of a priest was a recognized prerogative of Israelite leaders. Furthermore, Saul had a practical reason for acting on his own. While he waited for the tardy Samuel, the enemy had assembled its chariots on the plains below the Israelites' encampment, and Saul's aroused men were itching to get on with the fight. The situation posed a potentially serious morale problem that Saul had to take into consideration as commander and tactician. But when Samuel arrived on the scene too late to officiate, he was in no mood to hear such rationalizations; indeed, the old man was indignant. "You have behaved foolishly," he told Saul ominously.

One such disagreement might have been passed over, but there was more contention to come. The Amalekites, the tribe who traveled the desert southwest of the Israelites, attacked the Judean farmlands; and Samuel, speaking in the name of the Lord, ordered Saul to exterminate the raiders once and for all. "Go now and fall upon the Amalekites and destroy them," Samuel commanded. "Spare no one; put them all to death, men and women, children and babes in arms, herds and flocks, camels and asses." So Saul "cut the Amalekites to pieces," pursuing them all the way to the border of Egypt. But following his bent for mercy, he compromised with Samuel's instruction. He took the Amalekite leader captive and allowed his own men to seize as their customary booty "the fat beasts and the lambs and everything worth keeping."

Samuel soon heard of Saul's disobedience. He paid Saul a visit in camp, where the captured Amalekite livestock was all too clearly in evidence. "What," Samuel asked, "is this bleating of sheep in my ears? Why do I hear the lowing of cattle?" Saul lamely replied that the animals would not be distributed to his men but would be offered in ritual sacrifice. Samuel rebuked Saul further, announcing: "Because you have rejected the word of the Lord, the Lord has rejected you as king."

The sudden loss of the influential Samuel's support was serious enough for a king whose new-made office was not yet firmly established. But to Saul's difficulties in dealing with Samuel was added rivalry from his most talented subordinate, David, the youth made famous by his spectacular defeat of the Philistine strong man, Goliath. When the Israelite troops came home from witnessing that feat and from the mopping-up battles that followed, the news of David's personal triumph had preceded the army. Amid jingling tambourines, singing and dancing, "the women came out from all the cities to look on," the Bible recounts. But the merriment was sorry music to Saul's ears, for the women were singing: "Saul made havoc among thousands, but David among tens of thousands."

Saul had already shown himself vulnerable to violent emotions, and now that trait was to serve him ill. The feelings that overtook him as David's fame ascended were jealousy, spite and suspicion. He turned on David and tried to kill him, hurling his spear in David's direction while David sat strumming his harp for the king's amusement. He missed, David fled and Saul set assassins on his rival's trail. They did not succeed in catching up with David. The only effect of the pursuit, with which Saul became obsessed, was to build popular sentiment in favor of the dashing youth, who displayed neither fear nor spite, and who seemed unable to err except in the eyes of Saul. David reached his native hills of Judah, a safe distance from the increasingly agitated king. Meanwhile, Samuel, saying he had orders from the Lord, secretly anointed David as the future king of the Israelites —an act that would have exacerbated Saul's feelings still more had he known of it. As Samuel had foreseen, Saul lost the charisma so essential to his authority as leader. As his fortunes wavered, the Philistines saw their chance to launch a massive assault on the Israelites. They chose the valley of Jezreel, a swath of weakly defended territory. Saul rushed his troops to the scene of the attack, but he was too late; the Philistines slaughtered the Israelites, leaving thousands dead on the field—among them three of Saul's own sons. Saul himself suffered an arrow wound in the belly. Unable to flee and scorning the ignominy of captivity or death by a Philistine sword, he committed suicide.

The Philistines took cruel revenge. They cut off Saul's head and nailed his body, along with those of his sons, to the walls of the city of Beth-Shean. It was an ironic end for a man whom Samuel had triumphantly introduced to the people with the words: "Look at the man whom the Lord has chosen; there is no one like him in this whole nation."

Ornamented with three bands of worked gold, this 14th Century B.C. ivory horn was recovered from the ruined palace at Megiddo. In the 11th Century B.C., the judge Samuel used a similar vessel to pour the ritual oil anointing the head of David, designating him King of the Israelites.

But the story of Saul's stewardship, as recorded by Israelite scribes perhaps no more than a generation or two after his reign, is not a tragedy. Saul gave the Israelites what they needed at the time: a transitional figure who commanded the allegiance of all 12 tribes of Israel. It is also a magnificent literary chronicle, for Saul is a very lifelike hero. Human protagonists—as distinguished from gods as chief characters—had already appeared in literature; the Babylonian Gilgamesh was one. But Gilgamesh consorted with the gods on an almost equal footing, a flight of fancy that sets him apart from real life. Also, he and other literary figures up to this time were either unimpeachably good or irredeemably evil. The Bible presents Saul as quite a different sort—shot through with frailties as well as strengths.

To be sure, Saul suffered trials not of his own making: the esteemed judge Samuel emerges as a less than steadfast ally; David proves to be brash and, doubtless, an opportunist; and the Israelites, as subjects, are revealed to be both mercurial and stubborn. But those implicit facts serve as counterweights to the character of Saul, who in dealing with his problems is transformed before the reader's eyes from a conquering hero to a tormented one, from a promising if somewhat bashful youth to a spent man. As such, the portrayal of the Israelites' first king was something new in the annals of literature, by which the Israelites made a signal contribution to man's discovery of himself.

David fled from Saul's jealousy south into the hills of Judah, the home of his people, the tribe of Judah. But he was not a man to sit still. He made repeated expeditions through the countryside, gathering a band of followers around himself, putting down raids from nomads, even making temporary alliances with carefully chosen Philistines. In the process, he won a name for himself as a local protector of the people and established the power base that would enable him to assume the throne.

At Saul's death, David's own people acclaimed him "King of Judah"; significantly, they limited his jurisdiction to their own tribe. Nonetheless, all the other Israelite tribes to the north had reason to feel a strong pull of allegiance to him. To begin with, he had made no enemies among them. If David bore Saul any grudge, the younger man had discreetly kept it to himself. More than that, he publicly mourned the king's death. Thus Saul's supporters among the northern tribes found nothing for which to criticize David. Before long a deputation of elders came south to visit David at Hebron, where he had settled. "We are your own flesh and blood," they told him, referring to the Israelites' belief in their common ancestry. "And the Lord said to you, 'You shall be shepherd of my people Israel.'" And so, the story continues, "David made a covenant with them before the Lord, and they anointed David king over Israel."

David embarked on his reign at full tilt, exercising both military force and political acumen to make the most of his office both for himself and for his people, whom he now strove to unify more tightly than ever. He routed the Philistines once and for all, driving them west; henceforth they would be confined to a few cities along the southern coast. Inland he swept through all the surviving Canaanite cities, putting them under his own control.

His next move was to establish Jerusalem as his capital. It was a shrewd step. For David's purpose of reinforcing the unity of his people, the site was almost perfect. The city lay in the mountains, in neutral territory occupied by the Jebusites, a branch of a Canaanite clan; for the Israelites, therefore, it had no prior religious or proprietary associations. Yet Jerusalem was more or less central to all 12 tribes and near the boundary dividing the lands occupied by David's own tribe of Judah from the territories of Saul's tribe, the Benjaminites.

After seizing and occupying Jerusalem, David lost no time in supplying the city with the religious element he knew to be necessary for the conclusive welding together of his people. He brought to the city the Ark of the Covenant—recaptured from the Philistines, who had seized it in 1050 B.C., before Saul's time—and installed it in a sanctuary on a hill. For a people who had many shrines but no temple and no sacred images, the ark—the portable shrine that, the Israelites believed, housed the spirit of the Lord—was their one tangible object of veneration; by bringing it to his capital David gave the city sanctity, a powerful suggestion that the divine presence hovered at the royal doorstep. In effect, moving the ark to Jerusalem was a long step toward a secular monarchy free of dominance by priests and other religious spokesmen. David's control of the ark helped ensure that priestly elders would obey the king instead of giving him orders—a preeminence that would have served Saul well in dealing with Samuel.

Having secured his new base, David consolidated and broadened his power through astute diplomacy and an aggressive policy of conquest in territories beyond the Promised Land. He made an alliance with Hiram, King of Tyre; the most important outcome of that link was to be Israelite access to Tyre itself, one of the richest Mediterranean ports of the time. He subdued his immediate neighbors, making provinces of the kingdoms of Moab and Edom, where he installed Israelite garrisons. He exacted tribute from Ammon, whose king he allowed to remain in office as his vassal. He also stationed garrisons in Syrian territory extending some 60 miles north of the prosperous city of Damascus.

In the end, through this combination of garrisons and tribute-paying vassals in territories surrounding the Promised Land, David could claim an empire that stretched from the Sinai Peninsula almost as far east as the Euphrates River. For the first time, instead of living precariously in scattered patches of land that served as a communications corridor for foreign imperial powers, the Israelites had an integral state acknowledged by other powers.

By laying these political foundations, which were complete by about 975 B.C., David enhanced the value of the Israelite kingship, giving it the status of an enviable prize—and thus, ironically, created a severe problem of royal succession. The Israelites had never had a formal process for the selection of leaders. Tacit agreement among elders and popular acclamation had served during the era of the judges, but the judges were now in eclipse; the Israelites no longer had a Samuel to look to as the Lord's spokesman, and David now outshone his priests. As time passed and he himself made no designation of a future king, his numerous sons scrambled for advantage.

The likeliest candidate was David's favorite son, Absalom, who was in many respects much like his father. The Biblical story of Absalom's abortive attempt to wrest the monarchy from David sheds brilliant illumination on the primitive politics practiced in that era. It also marks yet another sophisticated developmental stage for Israelite literature; for the first time, the emotional pain of a ruler was described in broadly human terms.

Absalom had his father's thirst for adventure, and he was impatient. He might well have inherited the kingship on his father's death, but he was tempted to seek power early. Like David before him, Absalom moved independently and openly about the countryside, gathering personal supporters. Then, rashly, he marched on Jerusalem, bent on taking over the city and the kingdom by force.

He was no match for David, who had learned of the scheme and was far from ready to give up his throne. Absalom's eager recruits were easy prey for the king's men, a trained corps led by cool-headed officers. Their chief was a general named Joab, a bloodthirsty and arrogant intriguer who placed his own judgment in putting down the insurrection above that of his sovereign.

After an opening fray in which it appeared that Absalom had the upper hand, David mustered his army, gave the commanders orders to put down the rebellion and sent the troops off while he remained behind. As they departed, David had some final words of caution for his officers: "Deal gently with the young man Absalom for my sake." It was a command that all the men within hearing interpreted in only one way: bring back the rebel alive to face suitable punishment.

The king's men and Absalom's band came face to face in the forest of Ephron, a wooded region outside Jerusalem, where the pretender's forces suffered defeat. Oddly, the Israelites, perhaps alone among the powers of their time, had not yet adopted the horse

Text continued on page 112

Solomon's Fort at Megiddo

Occupying a strategic position at the head of a mountain pass and guarding access to the north from the coastal plain and Jerusalem, the city of Megiddo held an enduring importance as a fortress and center of commerce. Recent excavations of the site confirm that the mountain crest where Megiddo stood sustained a series of settlements for nearly 5,000 years, until the town finally fell to the Assyrians in 733 B.C. The largest and most completely preserved archeological layer, occupied around 1000 B.C., provides a view of engineering and construction techniques during the reigns of Solomon and Ahab. Architectural remains have enabled modern scholars in Jerusalem to build a scale model of the city as it looked during the Israelite monarchy *(below and overleaf)*.

Visitors entered Megiddo, as shown here in a detail from a model of the fortress city, by a ramp leading to the first of a complex of gates built during King Solomon's reign. The dimensions of the portal at top center —14 feet wide and 25 feet deep—exactly match the plans of gates elsewhere commissioned by Solomon, including a gate for the great temple in Jerusalem described by the prophet Ezekiel.

To provide secret access to a spring that supplied the city with water from a source outside the walls, Megiddo's engineers carved this 165-foot-long underground tunnel.

This site, long considered by experts to be the ruins of the stalls and feeding troughs in King Solomon's stables, is probably the remains of Megiddo's Ninth Century B.C. storehouses.

The portion of Megiddo that stood within the city's walls
occupied an area of 13 acres. The model, six and a half
feet square, shows the placement of the principal structures:
the palace at top center, storehouses at lower left, public
buildings at center and gate at bottom right. Private dwellings
must have clung to the outlying slopes, and in times of
danger the citizenry took refuge inside the fortification.

and chariot as a weapon of war; officers rode on donkeys. And as Absalom, thus mounted, advanced through the woods during the battle with his father's troops, he became entangled in the low-hanging bough of an oak tree. The donkey walked on riderless and Absalom swung in the air, trying in vain to free himself. Joab caught sight of him from a distance and, wantonly disobeying his king's command, picked up three sticks and flung them like arrows into the helpless Absalom's chest, knocking him senseless from the tree. Joab then dispatched his armor bearers to finish him off. With Absalom's death, the rebellion was finished.

Messengers to David preceded the returning Israelite army, and the king's first inquiry was for his son. Informed of what had happened, David, grief-stricken, went to the roof of his quarters, bowed his head and wept, "O Absalom, my son! my son!"

In this Biblical account of a father's bereavement, the image of King David assumed new royal dimensions—unlike the rigid, proud, invulnerable posture insisted upon by monarchs of other countries. Here was a mighty ruler brought low over the loss of an unruly and unseasoned son, an emotional predicament with which the humblest of David's subjects might identify.

But the pressures of statecraft ensured that the king could not nurse his personal feelings for long. His troops returned from the battle dismayed and stunned. They had witnessed Joab's flouting of a royal order and now, knowing of the king's loss, "they stole into the city like men ashamed to show their faces after a defeat in battle." All, that is, except Joab. Pitiless and arrogant, the general sought out David on his roof, upbraided him for failing to welcome "all

This 10th Century B.C. limestone altar, 22 inches high and from the Israelite city of Megiddo, matches one described in the Book of Kings. According to the scripture, the insubordinate general Joab, threatened with death for supporting a rival of King Solomon's, sought divine protection by entering the temple and clinging to the corner protuberances, or horns. The vestigial horns themselves may have been derived from the bull figures worshipped by the early Canaanites. Incense probably was burned atop the altar itself.

your servants who have saved you," and ordered the stricken king to "go at once and give [them] encouragement. If you refuse," he added, "not a man will stay with you tonight."

So David, rising from his deep anguish to meet his kingly responsibilities, went to the city gate and, silent but unreproachful, reassured his bewildered men by his presence among them. Thereafter, he bided his time before taking his revenge in stages. To begin with, David publicly stopped giving weight to the general's views. And then he assigned Joab demeaning or unpopular tasks far from the court, including census taking. In the end he advised his successor that Joab was not to be trusted.

"You know," David told Solomon, "how Joab son of Zeruiah treated me and what he did. . . . Do as your wisdom prompts you, and do not let his grey hairs go down to the grave in peace."

With that warning, David planted a seed that eventually led Solomon to order the general's execution. Meanwhile, it remained David's kingdom; none could doubt, nor could anyone challenge, his right to dispose of the realm as he saw fit. The matter of succession was at last settled toward the end of David's 40-year reign, when—with a little prodding from Bathsheba, his favorite wife—he designated Solomon, his son by her, to be his heir and ordered him anointed in public to certify the choice.

Solomon's reign brought the Israelites' new monarchy into full flower. He inherited a realm so secure that, except for putting down an inconsequential disturbance here and there, his army had little to do but keep watch by means of the kingdom's far-flung garrisons. Taking advantage of this situation, Solomon devoted his energies to internal development.

In Jerusalem, Solomon built the greatest monument to his rule: the temple to house the Ark of the Covenant, which until his time had stood in a modest tent. The Bible devotes more than eight pages to details of the temple's construction, furnishings and gala dedication. It was a marvel of cedar beams, cast-bronze pillars, ivory-paneled doors, golden vessels, and carved stone ornaments ranging from massive statues dominating the entrance to delicate sculptured flowers that graced the interior walls. Solomon also built a palace for himself and minor palaces nearby for the pleasure of the most favored of his reputed 700 wives, whose foreign origins and royal lineages expanded Solomon's room for diplomatic maneuver —especially in making alliances. The most celebrated of his wives was a child of the Egyptian pharaoh.

By this time, the Israelites had left their humiliation in Egypt far behind. Their fame was now almost universal. When the Queen of Sheba traveled from her realm in southwestern Arabia in order to pay Solomon a state visit, she told him: "The report which I heard in my own country about you was true, but I did not believe it until I came and saw for myself. Indeed I was not told half of it."

Outside Jerusalem, extending all across his kingdom, Solomon founded new cities and refurbished old ones. The gate that archeologists have excavated at Megiddo dates from his reign, as do the warehouses at Ezion-Geber, a port under Solomon's governance on the Gulf of Aqaba where goods of all kinds changed hands. From Ezion-Geber, some cargoes went west to Egypt and east to Arabia in ships provided by Hiram of Tyre. Other consignments traveled overland by caravan to the east. Solomon also capitalized on his father's alliance with Hiram to import the Phoenician monarch's craftsmen, who taught his own workmen the arts of carving stone and building ships; of mining, smelting, casting and hammering copper, bronze, silver and gold.

Solomon found innovative ways to increase his nation's wealth. He not only adopted the horse and chariot, which his father had ignored, but he also exploited them for commercial profit. The best chariots were built in Egypt; the best horses were bred in Cilicia, part of Anatolia. Solomon's kingdom lay directly between those countries, and it did not escape his notice that the empires on all sides of him found it necessary to import their mounts from Cilicia and their chariots from Egypt—just as he did. Solomon saw in this situation an opportunity for his people—and for himself—as brokers and traders, matching horses to chariots and buyers to sellers on a commission basis. The enterprise contributed considerably to the state's coffers.

Of all the undertakings of Solomon's reign, the crowning achievement was the beginning of that monumental creation of human literature on which this volume rests: the Bible. Scribes of David's court had set down some royal accounts, some narratives and some poetry; but scholars believe that it was in Solomon's time that the Israelites actually created in the books of Samuel the vivid, soul-searching, eloquent human portraits of Solomon's royal predecessors and the people in their lives. Just as epochal was the inception of efforts to compile the accounts that became, after many generations and many revisions, the books of Genesis, Exodus and Numbers. Before Solomon, the ancient stories had been as diverse and disparate as unsorted slides on a projector; for the

Jehu, a king of Israel, makes obeisance to the Assyrian monarch Shalmaneser III in this 10-inch-long detail from a basalt obelisk; Assyrian courtiers flank the two sovereigns. Shalmaneser commissioned the relief around 830 B.C., after Jehu peacefully submitted to Assyrian threats instead of defying them. Historians prize the scene because it offers the oldest-known identified portrait of an Israelite. Both kings are named in the inscription engraved on the monument.

first time man's perceptions—and his speculations about his origins—were to be assembled in a systematic and comprehensive way.

When Solomon died in 922 B.C. he left behind a kingdom vastly changed from the one Saul had inaugurated scarcely 100 years earlier. The population, by one archeologist's estimate, had doubled in that short time from 400,000 to 800,000. The court was opulent beyond Saul's imaginings.

But the gains of the kingdom had been won at the cost of a vast change in the social structure. Not all the national wealth could come from business ventures abroad or from tribute paid by vassals. Much of the state's income had to flow from the taxation of Solomon's own subjects. This method of raising revenue was exceptionally intolerable to the proud Israelites, who cherished a long memory of patriarchal days when every family was virtually a law unto itself; when the yield of a man's land was his own and he ruled his family with a free hand. There were Israelites still alive in Solomon's day who had first-hand recollections of the era of the judges—memories full of worrisome contrasts between the past and the present.

Life under Solomon suffered the impact of changes that affected every Israelite. The king divided the country into 12 districts, each with a governor who was responsible not to the tribal elders whom the people knew personally, but to Solomon and his court —a crowd of strange generals and bureaucrats who were necessarily remote from the people. One month of every year, each district was entirely responsible for providing the food, oil and wine that sustained the court. The requirement was onerous; according to the Biblical record, in a single day the court con-

sumed about 155 bushels of flour, over 300 bushels of meal, 10 fattened oxen, 20 ordinary oxen, 100 sheep, and an unspecified quantity of stags, gazelles, roebucks and fowl.

Besides contributing such provisions, the people were taxed through their muscle and sinew. Drafted work gangs cut and transported the great cedars, grown in Lebanon, that supported the temple and palace walls. Solomon levied 30,000 men from throughout the country and sent them to Lebanon in monthly relays of 10,000—each man being required to spend one month out of three away from home. That was a forlorn state of affairs for a people whose poetic ideal was to have "every man under his own vine and fig tree." And those numbers did not include another 150,000 who were pressed into service as quarriers, stone haulers and miners. In an ironic and agonizing parallel with an experience Israelites considered the most painful of their history, some of the Israelite work-gang superintendents lashed their human charges as indiscriminately as the hated foremen of Egypt had done in Moses' time.

Thus, at his death, along with all his accomplishments, Solomon left a people seething with resentment at forced labor and confiscatory taxation. Consequently, the gap between rulers and ruled widened. To these new problems were added a resurgence of disunity and separatism based on ancient geographic loyalties. The schisms were further deepened by new realities. Under the federalization instituted by Solomon, the north had assumed a specialized role: breadbasket of the kingdom, supplying the food for the south, which owed its power largely to trade.

Solomon's son Rehoboam succeeded him as king. He was an impolitic youth unable to deal with the crescendo of grumblings. His father's former counselors advised the young king: "If today you are willing to serve this people, show yourself their servant now and speak kindly to them, and they will be your servants ever after." But Rehoboam would not listen, and instead told his northern subjects, "My father made your yoke heavy; I will make it heavier."

The northern elders were outraged. "What share have we in David?" they exclaimed, remembering that their callow leader was the grandson of a man who had initially been acclaimed king only in the southern hills of Judah. "Now see to your own house, David," they said.

With those words the Israelites split into two kingdoms—a division Rehoboam's regime was too weak to prevent. The northerners chose a king of their own in Jeroboam, a former officer on Solomon's staff who was a member of the northern tribe of Ephraim; they called their new state the kingdom of Israel. The southern Israelites formed the kingdom of Judah— taking their state name from the tribe of Judah, from which name comes the word Jew.

The Israelite kingdoms were never to reunite politically. But as their people confronted new social problems, their religious life took on a new significance. Now it would not be kings who posed the questions and found the answers, but another group of men: the prophets. Fulfilling a role unique to the Israelites, the prophets' activities transcended political boundaries. Within 200 years after Solomon's death, the prophets were to begin crystallizing the people's common heritage and beliefs into a sophisticated, organized body of concepts that form the foundation of modern monotheism.

A Way of Life Shared with Friends and Enemies

After they moved into Canaan around 1200 B.C., the Israelites took up ways much like those of other settled Near Easterners. Ancient technologies differed little from place to place: farmers tended their crops; artisans spun yarn, hammered metal, threw pots, carved the instruments whose music brightened their days and gave expression to their faith. In time the Israelites' tribal structure was replaced by that of the clan, or *mishpahah*. These families became stratified between rich and poor—though there were no class distinctions and everyone in a given geographic area shared the same community rights.

There is no effective pictorial record of the Israelites' efforts during this time to master the principles of agriculture, the homely crafts, the arts of war. Nonetheless, it is possible to see reflections of their daily lives by examining the artifacts of their neighbors and their enemies, all of whom prolifically illustrated their own similar lives.

Using a method that began in the Third Millennium B.C., Israelite potters in Canaan shaped their wares on simple wheels, similar to the one being turned by this five-inch-high figure of an Egyptian artisan carved in limestone.

A Glimpse of Peaceful Pursuits

A woman of the Eighth Century B.C. kneads dough, made of meal ground daily from wheat or barley, in a typical three-legged trough. This pottery figure, three inches high, was found in a Phoenician grave at Achzib, near Tyre.

The peoples in the Land of Canaan must have bathed in this fashion—in large oval tubs filled with water brought from distant wells. Scholars speculate that the raised shelf in the tub facilitated foot washing. The three-inch-high sculpture, also found at Achzib, was made around 900 B.C.

Like the capable wife who, according to the Book of Proverbs,
"chooses wool and flax and toils at her work," a highborn
Elamite woman sits before a claw-footed table, winding wool
thread onto a spindle while a servant fans her. The Eighth
or Seventh Century B.C. relief, less than four inches high and
carved in bituminous stone, was discovered at Susa, in Iran.

Wheels and Mounts for a Mobile People

The design of this light spoke-wheeled chariot was already 500 years old when the Israelites entered Canaan. Around 950 B.C., King Solomon is said to have imported 1,400 of them, and the necessary horses, for use in combat. The 21-inch-high relief above was commissioned in the Ninth Century B.C. by the neo-Hittites, who used the vehicles not only in battle but, as here, for hunting lions with bow and arrow.

Canaanites of the 13th Century B.C. used this ceramic chariot, from a household tomb in Ugarit, as a votive offering. After assembling the model from fragments, archeologists fitted it with three objects uncovered nearby: two "passengers" measuring about six inches high and the head of a horse perched on a new wooden pole.

A Syrian warrior, mounted and
equipped much like the desert raiders
with whom King David did battle,
dominates this Ninth Century B.C.
limestone relief found in the palace of
Kapara at Tell Halaf. Besides use as
a war mount, the camel was the hardiest
pack animal in the Near East, capable
of hauling 500-pound loads more than 80
miles in one day. According to the
Bible, the boxlike saddle also served
as a hiding place for contraband.

Masters of the Martial Arts

King Solomon's charioteers engaged Aramaean cavalrymen like this warrior, who appears on this relief at the Kapara Palace. The sculpture reveals that these nomadic aggressors wore helmets, rode without saddles or stirrups and looped their shields over one shoulder to leave both hands free.

These two figures—an archer and a spearman—represent captives from Judah who were impressed into service as bodyguards to the Assyrian king after the capture of Lachish in 701 B.C. Their status is clear to scholars because, though members of the former enemy's army, they still wear typical Israelite headgear. This detail is from a stone relief, found at Nineveh, that portrays a military procession celebrating King Sennacherib's victory.

Conquering Assyrians beset the Israelites during the Ninth
and Eighth centuries B.C. This detail from a relief at the
palace of Ashurnasirpal II at Nimrud celebrates the king's
invincibility. His troops head for an attack on the far side of a
river, indicated by swirls. Two oarsmen, rowing a boatload
of supplies and equipment, are trailed by a groom swimming
beside a horse and by a warrior riding an inflated goatskin.

The Vital Role of Music Makers

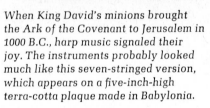

When King David's minions brought the Ark of the Covenant to Jerusalem in 1000 B.C., harp music signaled their joy. The instruments probably looked much like this seven-stringed version, which appears on a five-inch-high terra-cotta plaque made in Babylonia.

Canaanites paid homage to their deities with prayers set to music. These six-inch figures of musicians were modeled in the Eighth Century B.C. in the city of Achzib. One beats a tambourine; the other blows on the traditional double pipe, which makes an oboe-like sound.

A detail of an alabaster frieze found at an Assyrian palace offers particulars of other ancient musical instruments. These Seventh Century B.C. players are coaxing sounds from a drum, lyres —one with eight strings, the other with five—and a pair of small cymbals.

During the reign of King Solomon, the Israelites had for the first time enjoyed security, peace, prosperity and cultural growth. Now, after his death in 922 B.C., a series of mounting crises began with an internal split over succession and culminated in the wholesale uprooting of the people by foreign imperial giants. In that three-centuries-long process their faith was severely tested. But they reached a new perception of their own moral nature—the relationship of individual lives to issues of good and evil—and of the Almighty's role in relation to all human life.

That the land belonged to them by virtue of a sacred promise was axiomatic. But the period of crisis threw that axiom into grave doubt; as the Israelites' political structures began to show signs of strain, and as the brutal power of neighboring empires pressed in on them, the people came to perceive baleful inconsistencies in the allegiance of their god to them. In allowing victory to his people's enemies, the Lord seemed increasingly, and unfathomably, unreliable: at best, he appeared deaf to entreaties, at worst, powerless to protect the Israelites against the armies that ravaged the land and tormented them. How, they asked themselves, were they to sustain belief in a deity who was apparently capable of abrogating his side of a solemn bargain?

The Israelites found the answer in a reinterpretation of religious tenets. They achieved the new understanding partly by drawing on the spiritual capital of an ancient heritage, and partly by seeking fresh resources in moral concepts of their faith that they had not previously thought through.

All this was the work of a group of prophets: Amos, Hosea, Isaiah, Jeremiah, and perhaps a dozen others. The prophetic movement lasted a long time, from about 900 B.C. well into the Sixth Century B.C. But those who preached between 750 B.C., when the Assyrian Empire was just ascending, and 600 B.C., when its successor, the Babylonian Empire, was in its heyday, were the most important spokesmen to appear among the Israelites since the time of Moses in the 13th Century B.C.

Addressing themselves with ever-deepening gloom to the disasters befalling the Israelites, the prophets, through their strictures, introduced a revolutionary view of their god as controlling the destinies of *all* the world's peoples—not just their own. The dire warnings uttered by these men also, paradoxically, reaffirmed the Israelites' finest ideals: the pursuit of justice, mercy and love. The prophets built on these positive, basic tenets in stages and thereby enhanced appreciation of the purposeful benevolence of the deity in relation to those who worshipped him. In so doing they brought monotheism—which had gradually been taking form over the centuries—to its climax and readied the concept for transition to its final phase in Judaism, and later in Christianity and in Islam.

The political quarrels that soon after Solomon's death split the people into two kingdoms—Judah in the south, Israel in the north—resulted in two lines of rulers. Judah's monarchs traced direct descent from the dynasty of David, and could claim the ad-

A procession of Judean exiles—two women, two girls and a man leading an oxcart bearing two smaller children—sadly depart their home city of Lachish after its subjugation by Assyrian aggressors in 701 B.C. The refugee scene is a cast from just one panel of a bas-relief that was originally carved on a slab of gypsum. It was commissioned by the Assyrian tyrant Sennacherib to commemorate his triumph.

vantage of continuity. Israel's throne, lacking that base, was unstable. The kingdoms persisted side by side for about 200 years, until the Assyrians conquered Israel's capital at Samaria and deported the northern Israelites, scattering the population about their own empire. Judah survived alone until 587 B.C., when much of the populace was forced into exile in Babylonia.

In both kingdoms—despite division into two political states and despite intermittent quarrels—the people had remained powerfully linked by their common past. Each realm produced prophets whose messages, as recorded in the Bible, vividly reflect the political pressures on the kingdoms and the circumstances of daily life among all classes. These conditions have been corroborated to an astonishing degree by archeological excavations and by the written records of the peoples with whom the Israelites came into conflict. Nevertheless, despite the fascination of these political and domestic details, the real significance of the prophets' messages was spiritual; their words transcended national interests and outlived the contemporary political and social maladies they were meant to deal with.

The word "prophet" as used to describe certain Israelites of the Eighth and Seventh centuries B.C. does not focus on the ability to forecast events. To be sure, the gloomy predictions of the prophets seemed to be borne out with eerie accuracy. Their primary concern, however, was with the people's present conduct and its moral consequences. Their influence—and ultimate significance—derived from a talent for analyzing contemporary events and interpreting them to show that wrongdoing and corruption would inevitably result in political downfall.

That formulation of a moral imperative was an elevating new accomplishment for man. Indeed, these prophets were unique to the Israelites; no other society in the ancient world had seen their like. Other cultures—the Israelites included, for that matter—had honored their oracles. But such men were soothsayers and magicians who prognosticated good or evil fortune by using omens: reading the patterns made by flights of birds, or interpreting the shape of a dissected animal liver or the course of the stars. The Israelite prophets of the Eighth and Seventh centuries B.C. resorted to no such props. They relied on the inner voice of conscience that was already audible in the faith of their fathers. As self-designated spokesmen of the Lord's word, they reflected the older tradition of the judges, who spoke as conscience dictated and managed to influence their contemporaries solely by personal charismatic force. The observations of the prophets, however, were on a more sophisticated level; their views were more difficult to understand objectively and more difficult to listen to subjectively, arousing feelings of guilt after painful self-examination. Unlike the judges, therefore, the prophets were not consistently heeded.

Such is often the lot of visionaries who express themselves in sweeping terms. Nevertheless, in speaking the truth as they saw it, the prophets could be extremely persuasive when, as often happened, they addressed themselves to specific accusations of wrongdoing. This of course often meant defying the civil and religious authorities of the day: the king and his counselors at court, and the priests in the temples. The prophets railed against these powers for their hedonism, greed, falsehoods and idolatry, and for committing the sins of the flesh forbidden by the

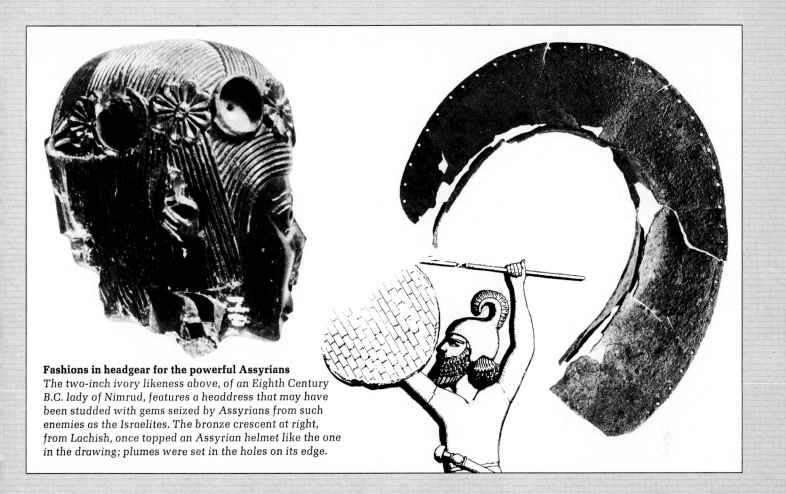

Fashions in headgear for the powerful Assyrians
The two-inch ivory likeness above, of an Eighth Century B.C. lady of Nimrud, features a headdress that may have been studded with gems seized by Assyrians from such enemies as the Israelites. The bronze crescent at right, from Lachish, once topped an Assyrian helmet like the one in the drawing; plumes were set in the holes on its edge.

Ten Commandments. They were not against monarchy as such, nor were they opposed to the temple and its rituals. (At least one prophet, Isaiah, claimed to have received his calling in a vision that occurred in the temple.) But the prophets did attack abuses that were being tolerated by both kings and priests. Indeed, most of the prophets looked back to David's reign as a model, and sought to resurrect that idyllic time by exhorting the people to mend their ways.

Appropriately enough, given their role as the Lord's spokesmen to all the people, the prophets represented a broad cross section of the now-multilayered Israelite society. They were a varied lot in their personal lives and marital status. Like the patriarchs, Amos was a herdsman—though he was also literate. Isaiah was a learned aristocrat, a husband and father, and possibly a nephew of King Amaziah, who ruled in Judah from 800 to 783 B.C. Jeremiah, a life-

long bachelor, was the son of a priest and possibly a descendant of Abiathar, one of the two priests whom David had put in charge of the Ark of the Covenant when he first moved it to Jerusalem. Hosea's occupation is not known, but he was by some interpretations married to a prostitute.

Amos was the first prophet whose writings have survived as a single book of the Bible. Born in the village of Tekoa, south of Bethlehem in Judah, he traveled north to preach in Israel—probably in Samaria, which in his time was the capital of Israel; certainly at Bethel, which in the 10th Century B.C. became a royal sanctuary under the first of the northern kings and where, according to tradition, Abraham had worshipped in patriarchal times.

Scholars date the time of Amos' activity to the decade between 760 and 750 B.C., since he himself speaks of preaching in the reign of Jeroboam II, who is known to have ruled from 786 to 746 B.C. Textual

Two naked priests—one holding a bowl with water to purify
the other's outstretched hands—crouch in a sacred grove. The
bronze sculpture, two feet long, was a personal shrine of
the King of Elam during the Second Millennium B.C. Found at
Susa, it probably replicates a rite dedicated to the sunrise;
cults that focused on celestial bodies flourished among
the Elamites in this period and, though forbidden to Israelites,
were followed by some as late as the Eighth Century B.C.

evidence places Amos' writings fairly late in that reign. He was active in a time of peace and overall prosperity, happier—at least superficially—than any span in either kingdom since the best years of Solomon's reign. But side by side with the riches enjoyed by some of the population went deepening poverty for others. The situation can be deduced from the rebukes Amos addressed to the wealthy classes and their way of life, and is borne out by archeological evidence. "Shame on you who live at ease in Zion," he said, referring to the mountain at the rich city of Jerusalem, where the temple stood and the rich of Judah regaled themselves. "And you, untroubled on the hill of Samaria," he said to their brethren of the kingdom of Israel, you "loll on beds inlaid with ivory and sprawl over your couches, feasting on lambs from the flock and fatted calves."

That Amos was not exaggerating the indulgences of the well-to-do in Israel is supported by evidence from excavations in Samaria, which have turned up the ruins of houses that were richly appointed with ivory furnishings. Archeologists have also discovered 63 fragments of inscribed pottery listing Samaria's palace inventory. They indicate lavish consumption, at the court, of wine and oil commodities that came as taxation from the kingdom's farmers, as did lambs and fatted calves.

Amos went on to level charges of outright dishonesty and heartlessness against the powerful and wealthy, accusing them of "giving short measure in the bushel and taking overweight in the silver, tilting the scales fraudulently." Worse, he said, "They sell the innocent for silver and the destitute for a pair of shoes" and "are not grieved at the ruin" of their less fortunate contemporaries. He was referring to the common practice of foreclosure by creditors of small farmers' properties and the selling into slavery of those who could not pay their debts.

Such haranguing of the rich for oppressing the poor may sound commonplace to modern ears, but it was revolutionary in the Eighth Century B.C. By prodding the social conscience of the more fortunate, Amos became the first prophet of record to argue that a people's fate is determined by the moral fiber of its society. Out of the economic injustice that he perceived in his time, Amos predicted the ultimate collapse of the Israelites, some three decades before the northern kingdom fell to the Assyrians in 722 B.C.

"An enemy shall surround the land," he told the people; "your strongholds shall be thrown down and your palaces sacked." At the shrine of Bethel he declared: "Your sons and daughters shall fall by the sword. Your land shall be divided up with a measuring-line, you yourself shall die in a heathen country, and Israel shall be deported far from their native land and go into exile." But Amos did offer some hope that these calamitous developments might be warded off. "Seek good, and not evil, that you may live," he advised the people; he also urged their leaders to "enthrone justice in the courts."

In all his preachings about the failings and wrongdoings of the rich and powerful—and the dire penalties to be paid therefor—Amos avoided blaming the king personally. Nonetheless, and not surprisingly, the authorities took Amos' words as seditious. He was expelled from Bethel by the high priest, who exclaimed, "Be off, you seer! Off with you to Judah!" Thereafter Amos evidently gave up preaching—but not without leaving a written record of his teachings.

When the people of the northern kingdom were in-

Text continued on page 136

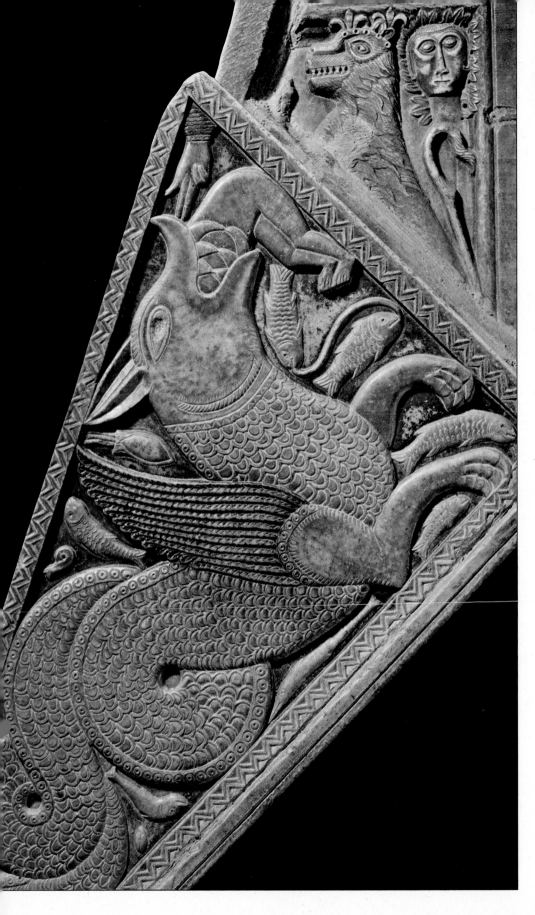

Jonah: A Fable of the Universal God

The 12 books of the prophets that conclude the Old Testament are short volumes. All but one are compilations of prophetic utterances and aphorisms. The exception is the story of the prophet Jonah, a parable set down around 400 B.C. to expound the moral that the Israelite god's protection and mercy extended to all people.

Jonah, symbolizing those who clung to the view that the Jews' religious legacy was exclusive, is charged by his god to warn the Assyrians that they must mend their ways or face doom. Unsympathetic, Jonah seeks to escape God's command by going to sea. But the Lord stirs up a typhoon and, to avoid disaster, Jonah volunteers to go overboard. He is thereupon swallowed by a monster. After three days Jonah is disgorged and reluctantly carries out the divine instructions; the Assyrians repent and, to Jonah's distress, are forgiven.

Medieval Christian artists saw the story as symbolic of the entombment and resurrection of Christ, and so illustrated it in many media.

Jonah disappears into a winged serpent in this marble carving, 54 inches long, made in 1260 A.D. for a church near Naples. Medieval artists, using Greek or Latin versions of the Bible as a source, rendered the big fish literally —as a sea beast, never as a whale. That mistranslation came from an English adaptation of the original Hebrew text.

Four men strain mightily at the oars as the others prepare to release Jonah into the open mouth of the eager sea serpent. Carved on a four-inch by 14-inch panel of ivory, the relief is one of many that cover a reliquary made in northern Italy in 360 A.D.

In one of the earliest and largest renditions of the prophet's tale, Jonah is suspended over the gunwale of the boat, on the verge of being engulfed by a long-necked, whiskered version of the monster. The scene—part of a 29-foot-wide mosaic on the floor of a church in Aquileia, Italy—was created in 314 A.D. The materials are cut stones, marble, glass and terra cotta.

A fragile-looking sailing vessel bobs in the waves next to the creature that is ingesting Jonah; the animal has leonine teeth and eyes and still manages a sharklike grin. This work, shown actual size, is one panel of an altarpiece at an abbey near Vienna. Made of enamel and gilt copper, it was done by a French artist in 1181 A.D.

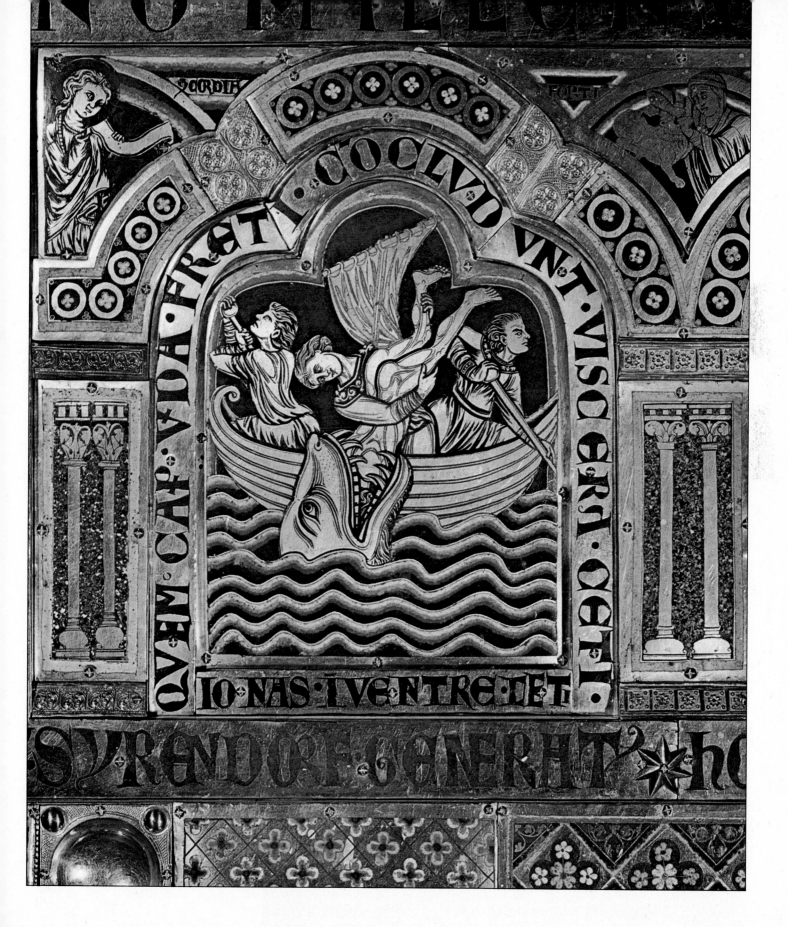

deed conquered, as Amos had foretold, his words appeared to have been clairvoyant. Yet any well-informed citizen of the time—and Amos was certainly an educated man—would have realized the ambitions of the great empires ranged on all sides of the Israelites. Once this fact was grasped, it would not have been difficult to analyze the political and military odds favoring the imperial aggressors.

At the time Amos spoke, the Assyrian Empire was on the eve of a new phase in its own history. Assyria was soon to inaugurate a succession of three of the most brutal rulers ever to stamp through human history: Tiglath-Pileser III, Sargon II and Sennacherib. Plundering, sacking, razing city walls and looting temple and palace halls, these Assyrian monarchs roared east, west and south out of Mesopotamia again and again for almost a century, beginning in 745 B.C. The Assyrian Empire was itself to fall to its southern neighbors, the Babylonians, toward the end of the Seventh Century B.C. But in its heyday, between perhaps 735 and 650 B.C., the Assyrian territory stretched from the mountains of Iran through modern Syria and Israel, past the old Philistine strongholds on the Mediterranean coast to the border of Egypt. For a while the Assyrians even made a vassal of the once-mighty empire of the pharaohs.

King Sargon II, though he accompanied his own forces into battle, found time on the march to record his exploits, some in the form of open letters to his national god Ashur. Some of these documents survive on steles—the stone tablets used by ancient conquerors to mark their rampaging progress—found at various points on the path Sargon trod between Iran and the Mediterranean. Along with wall inscriptions excavated at ancient city gates, the steles offer a chilling counterpoint to the plaintive wails of suffering that rise from the pages of the Bible.

Of his campaign in Israel, which brought the downfall Amos had predicted, Sargon boasted: "I led away as prisoners 27,290 inhabitants" of Samaria, and from the Israelite army he seized "50 chariots for my royal corps." Having done that, he went on to say—with the self-satisfaction of one who knows no doubts —that he rebuilt Samaria "better than it was before and settled therein people from countries which I myself had conquered."

For the vanquished the process of deportation and resettlement was one of the bitterest scourges of the Assyrian rise to power. The tactic was not an Assyrian invention, nor was it something new in imperial warfare, but the Assyrians made it their hallmark and practiced it savagely. Everywhere they went they rooted out all the upper classes—royalty, elders, craftsmen, merchants—removing them to one of their far-flung provinces. There, without loyalties or prerogatives, the deportees could cause no trouble. But their skills as financiers, administrators, architects, metalsmiths or scribes could be put to use in the interests of the ever-expanding empire.

The peasants who tilled the soil and the villagers of no account were left behind. But to keep them in line the conquerors installed Assyrian governors, along with a new upper class of people either from their own land or from some other conquered country —men whom they could completely trust to rule in the empire's name. These newcomers followed the ancient practice of bringing with them their own national gods—a development that somewhat accounts for the rising complaints against pagan practices voiced by the prophets over the ensuing century.

Assuming that Amos saw the external threat unfolding, his judgment might well have been strengthened by exchanging views with a like-minded prophet named Hosea. There is no evidence that the two ever met, but they were contemporaries. Hosea lived and preached longer than Amos—during the three decades between about 755 and 725 B.C. In that period Hosea added a new dimension to the Israelites' image of their god. His religious teaching contributed substantial elements of hope to offset the despair and defeat that he, like all the prophets, promised his people.

Much of Hosea's preaching took place at a time when the Assyrian menace was pressing ever closer upon Israel. The total destruction of the northern kingdom had not yet occurred, but in 733 B.C. the Assyrian armies destroyed the Israelite cities of Megiddo and Hazor, and left military overseers in charge of provinces carved from former Israelite land, stripping the kingdom of much of its territory. Surveying the wreckage, Hosea admonished his people, recalling the eagerness with which the Israelites had instituted their own kingdom some 300 years before: "Where now is your king that he may save you, or the rulers in all your cities for whom you asked?"

Like all the prophets, Hosea bitterly chastised those who could not see themselves and their fecklessness in its true light, saying, "A people without understanding comes to grief." He spared no one: "Hear this, you priests, and listen, all Israel; let the royal house mark my words. Sentence is passed on you." And of the faithful, who thought that blind observance of ritual would save them, he said: "They go with sacrifices of sheep and cattle to seek the Lord, but do not find him."

However, Hosea was not all hopelessness and reproaches. Indeed, a strongly positive note emerges in his preaching—a theme combined of love, mercy and trust. In Hosea's view the Israelite god was more than the jealous Yahweh of the Ten Commandments —though that element of divine character was still very much in evidence. This prophet perceived the Almighty as something more than a mere lawgiver who was immutably and punitively authoritarian: a repentant people could expect his protection as well as his forgiveness. Nonetheless, the price for absolution—and for avoiding punishment—was true faithfulness to the Lord.

Thus despite all their transgressions, Hosea held, the Israelites could aspire to regain their greatness if they would forswear foolish and self-destructive ways. He quoted the Lord as saying: "I will not let loose my fury for I am God and not a man"—thereby indicating that forgiveness is a divine attribute while vengeance lies to any human hand. "Turn back all of you by God's help," Hosea urged the Israelites, instructing them to "practice loyalty and wait always upon your God." And in a nostalgic note that looked back to a halcyon past, Hosea further quoted the Almighty: "I have been the Lord your God since your days in Egypt; I will make you live in tents yet again, as in the old days."

After the destruction of the northern kingdom and the deportation of its people to the east, the words of Amos and Hosea reached the south. There, during the reign of King Hezekiah, scribes are thought to have copied the manuscripts containing the two prophets' revelations. Hezekiah was able to inherit the kingdom of Judah largely because his father,

Ahaz, had fended off the Assyrian onslaught by stripping the temple of its gold and jeweled treasures to pay the first installments of the conquerors' tribute. Hezekiah subsequently levied a tax on the land-owners among his subjects to keep up the regular payments. Though the kingdom was reduced to vassalage, it nevertheless continued to prosper on a modest level.

After many years, Hezekiah saw a chance to skip the tribute at a time when Assyria appeared to be preoccupied elsewhere. But he miscalculated. Sennacherib, the Assyrian king, lashed back with a savage invasion of Judah. He stormed 46 of its cities, enslaved more than 200,000 people and captured the customary booty of horses, mules, camels, cattle, sheep and precious metals. He laid siege to Jerusalem itself, but failed to vanquish the capital. "As for Hezekiah," Sennacherib boasted, "himself like a caged bird I shut up in Jerusalem, his royal city." Sennacherib did not add that he had to head home because plague broke out among the men of his army —a fact reported in the Bible and later corroborated to some extent by the Greek historian Herodotus. So the kingdom of Judah, though diminished in size and population, still survived.

This was where the prophet Isaiah preached. A Jerusalemite, he was a firm believer in the divine covenant with David. He viewed his god as a divinely trustworthy figure who would in the end always intervene on behalf of the people, save them from oppression and establish a reign of righteousness. Isaiah, in other words, developed Hosea's themes of mercy and trust, and added to them a utopian view of the Israelites' future.

High idealism was the essence of Isaiah's vision; though hardly a joyful man, he was considerably less gloomy than his colleagues among the prophets. And Isaiah's faith in peace, expressed in a time of brutal warfare, is among the enduring paradoxes that have sustained the human spirit to the present day.

He did not doubt that some of the people, at least, would repent, and would abandon the sins of idolatry, venality, theft and licentiousness. He was confident that, despite the inexorable march of the ruthless Assyrians, a remnant of the Israelites would be spared the final punishment dealt the unrighteous. Given this fervent sense of his god's commitment to the well-being of the Israelites, it is not surprising that the passage most typical of Isaiah—and most frequently quoted—concludes with a trumpet call of hope for the nations of the world: "They shall beat their swords into mattocks and their spears into pruning knives; nation shall not lift sword against nation nor ever again be trained for war."

Isaiah's extraordinary vision also introduced a broadened and original view of the Israelites' god. It established their deity as the divine arbiter for the entire human world. In this universal approach, even the oppressor was cast as an adjunct of the Lord's power. "The Assyrian!" Isaiah said, quoting his god, "he is the rod that I wield in my anger, and the staff of my wrath is in his hand. I send him against a godless nation, I bid him march against a people who rouse my wrath."

With that passage Isaiah added a profound and far-reaching corollary to the view that the Israelites were suffering because they had disobeyed their god. Isaiah was arguing that the Assyrian tyrants under whom his people suffered were an integral part of the Israelite god's purpose for all men. "The Lord of

Text continued on page 143

The Horror of the Assyrian Onslaught

During the Eighth and Seventh centuries B.C., the Assyrians waged brutal campaigns to dominate the people whose territories surrounded their own. In Judah, the Israelite prophet Isaiah viewed the Assyrian menace as the expression of God's anger, and proclaimed that resistance was futile. Many Judean cities nonetheless tried to hold out against the relentless assaults—but in vain. When the city of Lachish finally fell in 701 B.C., Assyria's King Sennacherib commissioned bas-reliefs of the battle *(below)*. Later, Sennacherib's grandson commemorated his own military ferocity *(overleaf)*. The reliefs were copied by an English explorer who discovered the friezes at Nineveh in 1849.

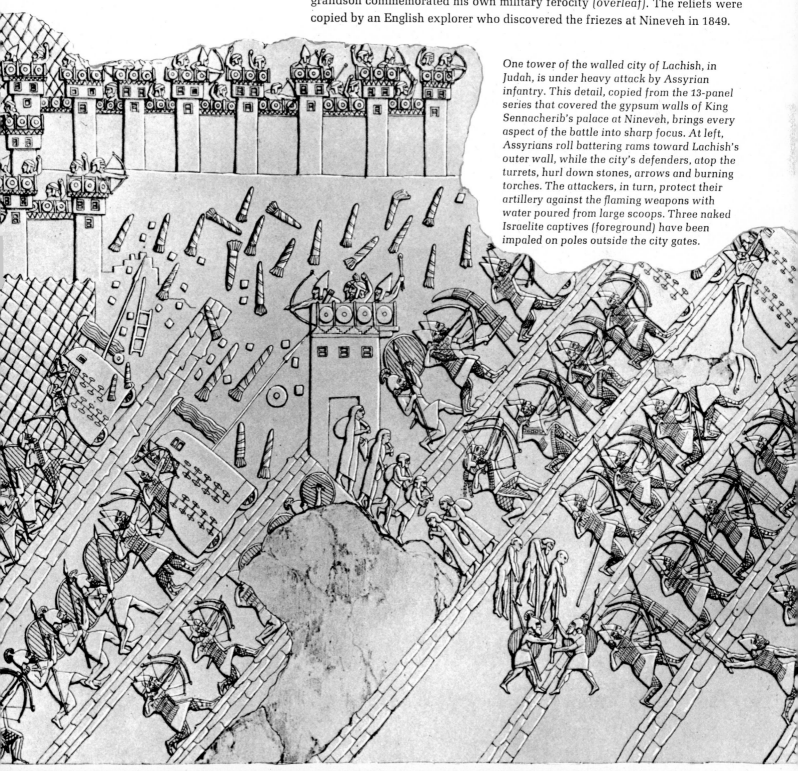

One tower of the walled city of Lachish, in Judah, is under heavy attack by Assyrian infantry. This detail, copied from the 13-panel series that covered the gypsum walls of King Sennacherib's palace at Nineveh, brings every aspect of the battle into sharp focus. At left, Assyrians roll battering rams toward Lachish's outer wall, while the city's defenders, atop the turrets, hurl down stones, arrows and burning torches. The attackers, in turn, protect their artillery against the flaming weapons with water poured from large scoops. Three naked Israelite captives *(foreground)* have been impaled on poles outside the city gates.

A Record of Torture and Mutilation

Inheriting the Assyrian tradition of merciless treatment for fallen foes, Sennacherib's grandson Ashurbanipal proudly recorded the post-battle atrocities following his own victory over the Elamites. He ordered a bas-relief carved for a palace at Nineveh to document his army's humiliation of the captives. In the top register of this detail two captives, with limbs staked to the ground, are being skinned alive. Below, one man writhes in agony as he is beaten with an iron bar; another, held by the hair, is having his tongue torn out.

On the fragment of another frieze from Nineveh, Assyrian soldiers, carrying severed enemy heads, pile the trophies before scribes who will count them.

Not even royal blood could move Assyrians to clemency. At the top left of this panel, the Elamite king draws his bow while his son kneels to beg for mercy. Later, to the right, the king is clubbed to the ground beside the prince's headless body. Finally, farther right, the king is decapitated.

Seated on an elaborate throne in front of his royal tent, King Sennacherib exacts tribute from his captives, the people of Lachish, in Judah. Above the king the cuneiform legend confirms the pictorial record: Sennacherib is receiving booty—mostly weapons of war—seized by his soldiers. The scene is accurately set in the hilly countryside outside the fallen Israelite city, where vineyards and orchards abounded.

Hosts has sworn," Isaiah told the Israelites, "this is the plan prepared for the whole earth, this the hand stretched out over all the nations."

A family god to Abraham. A tribal god to Moses and the judges. A national god to Saul and David and Solomon. Now, the god of the Israelites had become a god for peoples everywhere.

After Isaiah, the historical forces generated by invasion and internal division swiftly overtook the Israelites, and their political fortunes went into eclipse. Jeremiah, perhaps the most famous of the prophets and certainly the dourest, was on hand to witness the final blow to the Israelites. It came in 587 B.C., when the conquering Babylonians stripped Jerusalem and the kingdom of Judah of all their leading citizens and marched them off to Babylonia.

For the 50 years preceding that final cataclysm, Jeremiah preached the fundamental faith of the Israelites, based on the immemorial relationship between the people and their god. Jeremiah's personal contribution to the evolution of that faith, however, involved a new perspective of the ancient covenant. Henceforth, he declared, the words binding man to the Almighty would be written on the people's hearts instead of on tablets of stone. By accepting this instruction the Israelites could carry their religion with them anywhere, whether in bondage or in freedom; they could practice their faith without temples or religious symbols.

Jeremiah's concept linked the people's faith to their inner lives, particularly their private consciences. It also meant that worship could never be falsely observed and that it was a sin to go mechanically through the rituals. Jeremiah spoke out so strongly

on this subject that the authorities banned him from all public utterances within the precincts of the temple in Jerusalem.

The exhortation that excited this punishment is justifiably Jeremiah's most famous. He delivered the sermon in the fall of 609 B.C. or the winter of 608 B.C., shortly after the death of King Josiah.

Josiah had been a vigorous religious reformer, who abolished all the rural sanctuaries in an effort to centralize worship in the capital city and thus smother the paganism that tended to burgeon in the countryside. Jeremiah appears to have approved of the reformation in principle, but thought it had not gone far enough in practice. "You steal, you murder, you commit adultery and perjury, you burn sacrifices to Baal, you run after other gods whom you have not known," he told the people in the name of their god; "then you come and stand before me in this house," he went on, meaning the temple. "Do you think this house is a robber's cave?"

Though officially silenced after this speech, Jeremiah did not remain altogether mute. He dictated sermons to his friend Baruch, a professional scribe, who carried the texts on a scroll and, as Jeremiah's proxy, read them aloud at the temple. Baruch also recorded the book that preserves Jeremiah's words. It is a long work combining autobiography, biography, some poetry and some history—including Jeremiah's eyewitness description of the final burning of Jerusalem, the palace and the temple. It also contains what must have been a hearsay account of the grievous treatment dealt the last of David's descendants to hold the throne of Judah. According to the book, King Zedekiah was obliged by the Babylonian ruler Nebuchadnezzar to watch the flogging and execution of the royal family and the court, including Zedekiah's sons. Nebuchadnezzar then put out Zedekiah's eyes and had him led away to Babylon in chains.

Accompanying Zedekiah into the long exile were virtually all the males of Judah. "The captain of the guard," the book reports of the final rounding up, "left only the weakest class of people to be vinedressers"—that is, agricultural laborers. On that baneful note the kingdom of the Israelites ended.

But among the grandest epilogues of human history is the eventuality that the loss of their land —initially the very basis of the Israelites' sacred covenant, out of which grew all the other tenets of their faith—served to promote the expansion of monotheism. The Israelites in exile had no place to worship, and their own temple had been burned to the ground. But the spirit of their god no longer needed to be housed in a building: he resided in the human heart. That being so, the Israelites carried their identity with them, whereas the other peoples of their time depended for recognition on their geographical location or on their political singularity.

Unrestricted by national boundaries, the spiritual and ethical principles articulated by the Israelites spread slowly but steadily, developing further and being continually refined. The legacy of the Israelites still survives in the monotheistic religions that flourish today. All three faiths honor Abraham as the first spokesman of a binding covenant with the personal god they all worship. All three respect the written law summed up in the Commandments as stated by Moses. And all three venerate the moral and social ideals of righteousness, kindness, integrity and faithfulness first expressed by the Israelites.

The seminal conjuncture of these ideals represents an obligation, owed by the modern world to an otherwise obscure people, that can only be paid in the currency coined by the Israelites themselves: their faith that all men might one day live in a world ruled by the principles of peace, justice and love.

Summoned from the field by King David, Uriah the Hittite, with an attendant, is received by the ruler, who hoped to quell a royal scandal. Uriah's wife, Bathsheba, was carrying the king's child; David ordered the long-absent soldier to sleep with her. Uriah refused, went off to war—and death.

Three Great Sovereigns Who Made a Nation

The first three kings of the Israelites are among the earliest flesh-and-blood characters in the Old Testament's huge cast. Sufficient archeological and literary evidence has been accumulated to indicate that there was indeed a Saul, a David and a Solomon; and that the events of their lives—as recounted in the books of Samuel I and II and Kings—actually did occur much as described. Furthermore, the three regal figures who emerge from those pages certainly possessed the personal attributes, both weak and strong, given them by the scriptures' authors.

Annals kept by scribes in the Israelite court during the 10th Century B.C. provided much of the material in the Biblical accounts. Not every detail from the royal chronicles made its way into the scriptures, and later writers did embellish the facts and interject some parables. As a result, scholars have not been able to winnow all the fiction from the true history.

There were, as well, later imaginative contributors to the lore of the three sovereigns. Artists living long after the time of the Israelites—especially the Christian monks of the Middle Ages—translated the Bible's descriptions of the first kings into vivid illustrations for the sacred texts. Drawing inspiration from the words written in the First Millennium B.C., the artists portrayed Saul, David and Solomon in medieval dress and settings, as they appear on these pages.

During a rare respite from the battles that filled his reign, King Saul accepts homage from his men and urges them to keep fighting.

A Soldier Burdened by Tragedy

Saul, a soldier from the tribe of Benjamin, was designated first king of the Israelites around 1025 B.C. by the judge Samuel and the tribal elders. His entire reign was spent at war; he died as he had lived, fighting to expel the Philistines who invaded Canaan. But he was an authentic hero, whose victories—and defeats—became a constant theme of later Biblical paintings in which the image of Saul is always touched with sadness. He lost three of his four sons in battle and the surviving one was rejected by the Israelite people, so there was no heir-apparent to the throne. David, who was elected Saul's successor, outshone him both as a military commander and in personal charm.

In his final battle against the Philistines, at Mount Gilboa near the Sea of Galilee, King Saul (top right), with enemy barbs through his chest and head, falls on his own sword to avoid the humiliation of being taken prisoner.

A devout King David, in regal attire, strums a lyre accompaniment to one of the many psalms he composed in praise of the Israelites' god.

A lustful David spies Bathsheba in her tub and is enraptured. Shortly thereafter he summoned the lady, ordered her soldier-husband to certain death in battle, then married her.

Poet, Politician, Conqueror

David was a well-liked, multifaceted monarch whose 40-year reign was filled with accomplishments. He routed the Philistines from Canaan and expanded the boundaries over which the throne held sway. Through personal magnetism he joined the tribal confederacy of Judah with the kingdom of Israel and established a capital at Jerusalem, to which he carried the object most sacred to his people—the Ark of the Covenant. He was also an accomplished musician and a writer of poems and songs—including many of the Bible's psalms.

But the Bible records his foibles as well—among them his indulgence of Absalom, his rebellious son, and his love affair with the married Bathsheba. His son by Bathsheba—Solomon—succeeded him and brought the kingdom to its greatest glory.

A joyous King David, playing the zither-like psaltery, leads a procession of Israelites as they bear the sacred Ark of the Covenant into Jerusalem—the city David designated as the Israelites' capital. The date would have been around 1000 B.C.

Petitioned by two women, both claiming motherhood of the same child, the king suggests that the offspring be cut in two by a swordsman and shared. The woman who begged that the infant be spared, surrendering her claim, was then awarded the baby.

Builder, Businessman, Sage

Though the history of Solomon's reign is incomplete, many significant details are recorded in the Bible. To assure Israel's security, the king fortified the key cities—including Jerusalem, where he built a magnificent temple. To supply materials for his many ambitious projects, he saw to the development of vast mining and shipping operations; in the process of expanding trade, he inevitably embarked on new diplomatic ventures with neighboring peoples. He is also credited as the originator of the epigrams in the Book of Proverbs; and though he may not have been the first to utter them, many were certainly conceived at his court late in the 10th Century B.C.

The Queen of Sheba brings gifts to Solomon, seated on an ivory throne flanked by 12 gold lions representing the tribes of Israel. The visit was prompted by her wish for détente: the king's maritime fleet had been interfering with her trade routes.

The Emergence of Man

This chart records the progression of life on earth from its first appearance in the warm waters of the new-formed planet through the evolution of man himself; it traces his physical, social, technological and intellectual development to the Christian era. To place these advances in commonly used chronological sequences, the column at the

Geology	Archeology	Billions of Years Ago	
Precambrian earliest era		4.5	Creation of the Earth
		4	Formation of the primordial sea
		3	First life, single-celled algae and bacteria, appears in water
		2	
		1	
		Millions of Years Ago	
			First oxygen-breathing animals appear
		800	
			Primitive organisms develop interdependent specialized cells
		600	Shell-bearing multicelled invertebrate animals appear
Paleozoic ancient life			Evolution of armored fish, first animals to possess backbones
		400	Small amphibians venture onto land
			Reptiles and insects arise
			Thecodont, ancestor of dinosaurs, arises
Mesozoic middle life		200	Age of dinosaurs begins
			Birds appear
			Mammals live in shadow of dinosaurs
			Age of dinosaurs ends
		80	
			Prosimians, earliest primates, develop in trees
Cenozoic recent life		60	
		40	Monkeys and apes evolve
		20	
		10	Ramapithecus, oldest known primate with apparently manlike traits, evolves in India and Africa
		8	
		6	
		4	Australopithecus, closest primate ancestor to man, appears in Africa

Geology	Archeology	Millions of Years Ago	
Lower Pleistocene oldest period of most recent epoch	**Lower Paleolithic** oldest period of Old Stone Age	2	Oldest known tool fashioned by man in Africa
		1	First true man, Homo erectus, emerges in East Indies and Africa
			Homo erectus populates temperate zones
		Thousands of Years Ago	
Middle Pleistocene middle period of most recent epoch		800	Man learns to control and use fire
		600	
			Large-scale, organized elephant hunts staged in Europe
		400	Man begins to make artificial shelters from branches
		200	
Upper Pleistocene latest period of most recent epoch	**Middle Paleolithic** middle period of Old Stone Age		Neanderthal man emerges in Europe
		80	
		60	Ritual burials in Europe and Near East suggest belief in afterlife
			Woolly mammoths hunted by Neanderthals in northern Europe
		40	Cave bear becomes focus of cult in Europe
	Upper Paleolithic latest period of Old Stone Age		Cro-Magnon man arises in Europe
			Asian hunters cross Bering Land Bridge to populate New World
			Oldest known written record, lunar notations on bone, made in Europe
			Man reaches Australia
			First artists decorate walls and ceilings of caves in France and Spain
		30	Figurines sculpted for nature worship
		20	Invention of needle makes sewing possible
			Bison hunting begins on Great Plains of North America
Holocene present epoch	**Mesolithic** Middle Stone Age	10	Bow and arrow invented in Europe
			Pottery first made in Japan

(Last Ice Age — spanning Upper Pleistocene through Upper Paleolithic)

▼ Four billion years ago   ▼ Three billion years ago

▲ Origin of the Earth (4.5 billion)   ▲ First life (3.5 billion)

left of each of the chart's four sections identifies the great geo-
gical eras into which the earth's history is divided by scientists,
while the second column lists the archeological ages of human his-
ory. The key dates in the rise of life and of man's outstanding
ccomplishments appear in the third column (years and events mentioned in this volume of The Emergence of Man appear in bold type).
The chart is not to scale; the reason is made clear by the bar below,
which represents in linear scale the 4.5 billion years spanned by the
chart—on the scaled bar, the portion relating to the total period of
known human existence (far right) is too small to be distinguished.

Geology	Archeology	Years B.C.	
Holocene (cont.)	Neolithic New Stone Age	9000	
			Sheep domesticated in Near East
			Dog domesticated in North America
		8000	Jericho, oldest known city, settled
			Goat domesticated in Persia
			Man cultivates his first crops, wheat and barley, in Near East
		7000	Pattern of village life grows in Near East
			Catal Hüyük, in what is now Turkey, becomes largest Neolithic city
			Loom invented in Near East
			Cattle domesticated in Near East
		6000	Agriculture begins to replace hunting in Europe
			Copper used in trade in Mediterranean area
	Copper Age		Corn cultivated in Mexico
		4800	Oldest known massive stone monument built in Brittany
		4000	Sail-propelled boats used in Egypt
			First city-states develop in Sumer
			Cylinder seals begin to be used as marks of identification in Near East
		3500	First potatoes grown in South America
			Wheel originates in Sumer
			Man begins to cultivate rice in Far East
			Silk moth domesticated in China
			Horse domesticated in south Russia
			Egyptian merchant trading ships start to ply the Mediterranean
			Pictographic writing invented in Near East
	Bronze Age	3000	Bronze first used to make tools in Near East
			City life spreads to Nile Valley
			Plow is developed in Near East
			Accurate calendar based on stellar observation devised in Egypt
		2800	Stonehenge, most famous of ancient stone monuments, begun in England
			Pyramids built in Egypt
		2600	Variety of gods and heroes glorified in Gilgamesh and other epics in Near East

Geology	Archeology	Years B.C.	
Holocene (cont.)	Bronze Age (cont.)	2500	Cities rise in the Indus Valley
			Earliest evidence of use of skis in Scandinavia
			Earliest written code of laws drawn up in Sumer
		2000	Minoan palace societies begin on Crete
			Use of bronze in Europe
			Chicken and elephant domesticated in Indus Valley
			Eskimo culture begins in Bering Strait area
		1500	Invention of ocean-going outrigger canoes enables man to reach islands of South Pacific
			Ceremonial bronze sculptures created in China
			Imperial government, ruling distant provinces, established by Hittites
		1400	Iron in use in Near East
			First complete alphabet devised in script of the Ugarit people in Syria
			Moses leads Israelites out of Egypt
	Iron Age	1000	Reindeer domesticated in Eurasia
			Phoenicians spread alphabet
		900	
		800	Use of iron begins to spread throughout Europe
			First highway system built in Assyria
			Homer composes Iliad and Odyssey
			Mounted nomads appear in the Near East as a new and powerful force
			Rome founded
		700	Etruscan civilization in Italy
			Cyrus the Great rules Persian Empire
		500	Roman Republic established
			Wheel barrow invented in China
		200	Epics about India's gods and heroes, the Mahabharata and Ramayana, written
			Water wheel invented in Near East
		0	Christian era begins

▼ Two billion years ago   ▼ One billion years ago

First oxygen-breathing animals (900 million) ▲   First animals to possess ▲   First men (1.3 million) ▲
backbones (470 million)

Credits

Credits from left to right are separated by semicolons, from top to bottom by dashes.

All quotations are from *The New English Bible* © the Delegates of the Oxford University Press and the Syndics of the Cambridge University Press, 1961, 1970. Reprinted by permission.

Cover—Painting by Burt Silverman, background photograph by David Lees, from TIME-LIFE Picture Agency. 8—Ted Spiegel from Black Star. 12, 13—Maps by Rafael D. Palacios. 15—Courtesy of the Trustees of the British Museum, London. 16, 17—David Harris, photographed and exhibited in the Israel Museum, from the collections of the Israel Department of Antiquities and Museums. 18, 19—Derek Bayes courtesy the British Museum (Natural History), except center, Eileen Tweedy courtesy the British Museum (Natural History). 21, 22, 23—David Harris. 27—Graham Finlayson from Woodfin Camp and Associates. 28—David Harris. 29—James Whitmore, from TIME-LIFE Picture Agency. 30—David Harris courtesy Shrine of the Book, the Israel Museum, Jerusalem; David Harris. 31—Courtesy Shrine of the Book, the Israel Museum, Jerusalem. 32—David Rubinger, from TIME-LIFE Picture Agency. 33—Eliot Elisofon courtesy Eliot Elisofon Estate. 34—Erich Lessing from Magnum courtesy Musée du Louvre, Paris. 38, 39—David Lees, from TIME-LIFE Picture Agency. 40—David Lees. 42—Courtesy Jericho Excavation Fund. 44 through 47—Drawings by Michael A. Hampshire. 49—Erich Lessing from Magnum. Copy by E. Weidenbach from tomb of Chnum-Hotep in Beni Hasan, Kunsthistorisches Museum, Vienna. 50—Fred Anderegg in *Jewish Symbols in the Greco-Roman Period* by Erwin R. Goodenough, Bollingen Series XXXVII, copyright © 1964 Bollingen Foundation. Reproduced by permission of Princeton University Press. 52—Erich Lessing from Magnum. Tomb of Menna, scribe of Thutmose IV, Thebes. 54, 55—Brian Brake from Rapho Guillumette courtesy Egyptian Museum, Cairo. 56—Courtesy of The Brooklyn Museum: Charles Edwin Wilbour Fund; Bildarchiv Foto Marburg courtesy Egyptian Museum, Cairo; The Walters Art Gallery. 57

—Courtesy of The Brooklyn Museum; The Metropolitan Museum of Art, photograph by Harry Burton. 58, 59—Fred Anderegg in *Jewish Symbols in the Greco-Roman Period* by Erwin R. Goodenough, Bollingen Series XXXVII, copyright © 1964 Bollingen Foundation. Reproduced by permission of Princeton University Press. 62—Archiv für Kunst und Geschichte courtesy Roemer-Pelizaeus Museum, Hildesheim—Hirmer Fotoarchiv, Munich courtesy The Iraq Museum, Baghdad. 63—Erich Lessing from Magnum courtesy Musée du Louvre, Paris. 66, 67—Dmitri Kessel courtesy Cabinet des Estampes, Bibliothèque Nationale, Paris. 69—Map by Rafael D. Palacios based on a map in the *Encyclopaedia Judaica*. All maps pages 70 through 76 are by Rafael D. Palacios. 70, 71, 72—David Harris. 73—David Harris—David Lees, from TIME-LIFE Picture Agency. 74, 75—David Harris. 76, 77—David Lees, from TIME-LIFE Picture Agency. 78—Frank J. Scherschel, from TIME-LIFE Picture Agency courtesy of the Oriental Institute, University of Chicago. 80, 81—Scala courtesy the Baptistery, Florence Cathedral. 82—Map by Rafael D. Palacios. 84—Professor Yigael Yadin courtesy Hazor Museum. 85—Professor Yigael Yadin; Floor plan adapted from a drawing in *Encyclopedia of Archeological Excavations in the Holy Land*, Vol. I, 1970, p.162. 87—Erich Lessing from Magnum courtesy of the Israel Department of Antiquities and Museums. 89—David Harris, photographed and exhibited in the Israel Museum, from the collections of the Israel Department of Antiquities and Museums. 90—Erich Lessing from Magnum. Temple of Ramses III at Medinet Habu. 93 through 99—Drawings by Michael A. Hampshire. 100—Dr. Georg Gerster from Rapho Guillumette. 103—Erich Lessing from Magnum, photographed from a plaster cast courtesy of the Israel Department of Antiquities and Museums. Original in the British Museum, London—Courtesy of the Trustees of the British Museum, London. 106—Erich Lessing from Magnum courtesy of the Israel Department of Antiquities and Museums. 109—Werner Braun courtesy Megiddo Museum. 110, 111—Courtesy of the Oriental Institute, University of Chicago; Werner Braun courtesy Megiddo Museum. 112—David Harris, photographed and exhib-

ited in the Israel Museum, from the collections of the Israel Department of Antiquities and Museums. 114—Courtesy of the Trustees of the British Museum, London. 117—Courtesy of the Oriental Institute, University of Chicago. 118—Courtesy of the Israel Department of Antiquities and Museums—Erich Lessing from Magnum courtesy of the Israel Department of Antiquities and Museums. 119—Archives Photographiques courtesy the Department of Oriental Antiquities, Musée du Louvre, Paris. 120—Giraudon courtesy the Department of Oriental Antiquities, Musée du Louvre, Paris. 121—The Walters Art Gallery. 122—Bildarchiv Foto Marburg courtesy Vorderasiatisches Museum, Berlin; Courtesy of the Trustees of the British Museum, London. 123—Giraudon courtesy of the Trustees of the British Museum, London. 124—Erich Lessing from Magnum courtesy of the Israel Department of Antiquities and Museums; Courtesy of the Oriental Institute, University of Chicago. 125—Archives Photographiques courtesy Musée du Louvre, Paris. 126—Erich Lessing from Magnum, photographed from a plaster cast courtesy of the Israel Department of Antiquities and Museums. Original in the British Museum, London. 129—From *Nimrud and Its Remains* by Sir Max Mallowan, William Collins Sons and Co., Ltd., 1966; Courtesy of the Israel Department of Antiquities and Museums—Drawing from *Monuments de Ninive*, Vol. II by P. E. Botta and Flandin, Paris, 1849, Plate 147. 130, 131—Erich Lessing from Magnum courtesy Musée du Louvre, Paris. 133—Scala courtesy the Cathedral of San Pietro, Minturno. 134—Scala courtesy Museo Cristiano, Brescia—Scala courtesy the Basilica, Aquileia. 135—Erich Lessing from Magnum courtesy Stift Klosterneuburg, Austria. 139 through 142—Paulus Leeser courtesy Oriental Division, The New York Public Library, Astor, Lenox and Tilden Foundations. 145—Bulloz courtesy Musée du Petit-Palais, Paris. 146, 147—Courtesy The Pierpont Morgan Library, M. 638, ff. 23 and 34v. 148—Scala courtesy the Cathedral, Cividale del Friuli. 149—Bulloz courtesy Musée du Petit-Palais, Paris; Ann Münchow courtesy Staatsbibliothek Preussischer Kulturbesitz, Berlin. 150—The British Library. 151—Denise Bourbonnais courtesy Musée Condé de Chantilly.

Acknowledgments

For the help given in the preparation of this book, the editors are indebted to Pierre Amiet, Chief Curator, Department of Oriental Antiquities, Louvre Museum; Aline Bassot, Assistant Librarian, Bibliothèque Municipale, Moulins; Brigitte Baumbusch, Florence; Catherine Bélanger, Louvre Museum; Denise Bourbonnais, Paris; Luigi Capuano, Tourist Agency, Minturno, Italy; Annie Caubet, Curator, Department of Oriental Antiquities, Louvre Museum; Madelin Caviness, Lexington, Massachusetts; Raymond Cazelle, Curator of Collections, Musée Condé de Chantilly; P. I. Edwards, Department of Botany, the British Museum (Natural History), London; Pierre Gasnault, Curator, Department of Manuscripts, Bibliothèque Nationale, Paris; Béatrice el Habib, Curator, Musée du Petit-Palais, Paris; David Harris, Jerusalem; Monsignor Luigi Marcuzzi, Basilica of the Assumption of Mary, Aquileia, Italy; Francine Masson, Curator of the Comte Robert du Mesnil du Buisson, Paris; Gerhard Rudolf Meyer, Professor Dr., Near Eastern Department, State Museum of Berlin, East Berlin; T. C. Mitchell, Department of Asiatic Antiquities, the British Museum, London; Tony Rees, London; J. Rosenwasser, Department of Oriental Printed Books, the British Museum, London; C. F. A. Schaeffer, French Institute, Paris; Françoise Tallon, Researcher, Department of Oriental Antiquities, Louvre Museum; Gabrielle de Witwicki, Musée Condé de Chantilly.

Bibliography

Aharoni, Yohanan, and Michael Avi-Yonah, *The Macmillan Bible Atlas*. The Macmillan Company, 1972.

Amiran, Ruth, *Ancient Pottery of the Holy Land*. Rutgers University Press, 1970.

Anati, Emmanuel, *Palestine before the Hebrews*. Alfred A. Knopf, 1963.

Au-Yonah, Michael, and Emil Kraeling, *Our Living Bible*. McGraw-Hill, 1962.

Beek, Martin A., *Atlas of Mesopotamia*. Translated from the Dutch by D. R. Welsh. Thomas Nelson and Sons Limited, 1962.

Bottéro, Jean, Elena Cassin, and Jean Vercoutter, eds., *The Near East: The Early Civilizations*. Translated from the French by R. F. Tannenbaum. Delacorte Press, 1967.

Bright, John, *A History of Israel*. Westminster Press, 1959.

De Vaux, Roland, *Ancient Israel*. Translated from the French by John McHugh. McGraw-Hill Book Company, n.d.

Edwards, I. E. S., C. J. Gadd, N. G. L. Hammond, E. Sollberger, eds., *The Cambridge Ancient History*, Vol. II. Cambridge University Press, 1973.

Ellison, John, *Nelson's Complete Concordance of the Revised Standard Version Bible*. Thomas Nelson & Sons, 1957.

Encyclopaedia Judaica. Keter Publishing House Ltd., 1972.

Erman, Adolf:
ed., *The Ancient Egyptians*. Harper & Row, 1966.
Life in Ancient Egypt. Dover Publications, 1971.

Farb, Peter, *The Land, Wildlife, and Peoples of the Bible*. Harper & Row, 1967.

Frank, Henry Thomas, *Bible, Archaeology and Faith*. Abingdon Press, 1971.

Frankfort, Henri, *Kingship and the Gods*. The University of Chicago Press, 1948.

Frankfort, H. and H. A., John A. Wilson, Thorkild Jacobsen, William A. Irwin, *The Intellectual Adventure of Ancient Man*. The University of Chicago Press, 1946.

Gardner, Sir Alan, *Egypt of the Pharaohs*. Oxford University Press, 1961.

Gaster, Theodor H., *Myth, Legend and Custom in the Old Testament*. Harper & Row, 1969.

Gehman, Henry Snyder, ed., *The New Westminster Dictionary of the Bible*. Westminster Press, 1970.

Ghirshman, R., *Iran*. Penguin Books, 1954.

Gray, George Buchanan, *Sacrifice in the Old Testament*. KTAV Publishing House, Inc., 1971.

Gray, John, *The Canaanites*. Frederick A. Praeger, 1964.

Heidel, Alexander, *The Gilgamesh Epic and Old Testament Parallels*. The University of Chicago Press, 1946.

Holt, John M., *The Patriarchs of Israel*. Vanderbilt University Press, 1964.

Jacobsen, Thorkild, *Toward the Image of Tammuz*. Harvard University Press, 1970.

Jastrow, Morris, *Aspects of Religious Belief in Babylonia and Assyria*. Benjamin Blom, Inc., 1971.

Kaufmann, Yehezkel, *The Religion of Israel*. Translated and abridged by Moshe Greenberg. University of Chicago Press, 1960.

Kees, Hermann, *Ancient Egypt*. Translated from the German by Ian F. D. Morrow. Faber and Faber, 1961.

Kenyon, Kathleen M.:
Archaeology in the Holy Land. Praeger Publishers, 1970.
Digging Up Jericho. Ernest Benn Limited, 1957.

Landay, Jerry M., *Silent Cities, Sacred Stones*. McCall Publishing Co., 1971.

Lange, Kurt, and Max Hirmer, *Egypt*. Translated from the German by R. H. Boothroyd, Judith Filson and Barbara Taylor. Phaidon Press, 1968.

Mazar, B., ed., *World History of the Jewish People: Patriarchs* (Vol. II) and *Judges* (Vol. III). Rutgers University Press, 1970, 1971.

Moller-Christensen, V., and K. E. Jorgensen, *Encyclopedia of Bible Creatures*. Fortress Press, 1965.

Montet, Pierre, *Eternal Egypt*. Translated from the French by Doreen Weightman. The New American Library, 1964.

Moscati, Sabatino:
The Face of the Ancient Orient. Anchor Books, 1962.
The World of the Phoenicians. Translated from the Italian by Alastair Hamilton. Frederick A. Praeger, 1968.

Netanyahu, B., and E. A. Speiser, eds., *World History of the Jewish People: At the Dawn of Civilization* (Vol. I). Rutgers University Press, 1964.

Noth, Martin, *The History of Israel*. Harper & Row, 1960.

Oesterley, W. O. E., *Sacrifices in Ancient Israel*. Hodder and Stoughton, 1937.

Oppenheim, A. Leo, *Ancient Mesopotamia*. The University of Chicago Press, 1964.

Pearlman, Moshe, *Moses*. Abelard-Schuman Limited, 1974.

Pritchard, James B.:
The Ancient Near East in Pictures. Princeton University Press, 1969.
ed., *Ancient Near Eastern Texts*. Princeton University Press, 1955.

Rothenberg, Beno, *God's Wilderness*. Thomas Nelson and Sons, 1962.

Saggs, H. W. F., *The Greatness That Was Babylon*. Hawthorn Books, Inc., 1972.

Sandmel, Samuel, *The Hebrew Scriptures*. Alfred A. Knopf, 1963.

Smith, Morton, *Palestinian Parties and Politics That Shaped the Old Testament*. Columbia University Press, 1971.

Ucko, Peter J., and G. W. Dimbleby, eds., *The Domestication and Exploitation of Plants and Animals*. Aldine Publishing Co., 1969.

Van Deurgen, A., *Illustrated Dictionary of Bible Manners and Customs*. Zondervan Publishing House, 1958.

Wilson, John A., *The Culture of Ancient Egypt*. The University of Chicago Press, 1951.

Wiseman, D. J., ed., *Peoples of Old Testament Times*. Oxford University Press, 1973.

Wright, G. Ernest, *Biblical Archaeology*. Westminster Press, 1957.

Wright, G. Ernest, and David Noel Freedman, eds., *The Biblical Archaeologist Reader*. Anchor Books, 1971.

Yadin, Yigael, *Hazor*. Oxford University Press, 1972.

Index

Numerals in italics indicate an illustration of the subject mentioned.